The Giant Book of Unusual Facts

By
Jake Jacobs

Kindle Edition

* * * * *

Published by Jake Jacobs at Amazon Kindle

1.

Great Value Ice Cream Sandwiches don't melt because of their structural integrity.

Reference: (https://www.snopes.com/fact-check/great-value/)

2.

Most coins were made using something called a Janvier Reducing Machine. Large versions of the coin were made, then the machine would trace the relief and translate the movements to engrave a die in the coins desired size.

Reference: (http://www.royalmintmuseum.org.uk/Blog/object-in-focus-janvier-reducing-machine)

3.

The Lehigh Tunnel in Pennsylvania's two tubes were dug using different methods; as a result, one is circular and the other is rectangular.

Reference: (https://en.wikipedia.org/wiki/Lehigh_Tunnel)

4.

The U.S. Navy replaced expensive and clunky periscope controls on submarines with Xbox 360 controllers, which reduced training time from hours to minutes.

Reference: (https://www.theverge.com/2017/9/19/16333376/us-navy-military-xbox-360-controller)

5.

The tobacco smoke enema was a medical procedure used during the colonial age to treat stomach pains and to revive drowning victims. It involves forcing tobacco smoke into the patient's rectum.

Reference: (https://en.wikipedia.org/wiki/Tobacco_smoke_enema)

6.

Bruce Lee had the sweat glands in his armpits removed, which may have actually led to his death due to overheating.

Reference: (https://www.yahoo.com/entertainment/did-bruce-lee-die-book-sad-strange-explanation-174047828.html)

7.

The 27 kilometer Large Hadron Collider shrinks by 30 meters in size, once the liquid helium is put inside of it.

Reference: (https://youtu.be/edvdzh9Pggg?t=36m50s)

8.

Heart Attack Grill is a Las Vegas restaurant where people over 350 pounds eat for free. 3 people have died while eating there, and the only vegan option on their menu is cigarettes.

Reference:
(https://en.wikipedia.org/wiki/Heart_Attack_Grill#Deaths)

9.

The man who killed John Wilkes Booth was an eccentric religious fanatic who castrated himself before enlisting in the Union Army.

Reference: (http://www.newenglandhistoricalsociety.com/boston-corbett-mad-hatter-killed-john-wilkes-booth/)

10.

In 1913 and 1914, it was legal in the U.S. to mail children under 50 pounds.

Reference: (https://en.wikipedia.org/wiki/Human_mail)

11.

When BET aired showings of The Wire Season 2, the dock workers story line was almost completely edited out compared to the drug dealers story line in the city. It is unknown if it was for racial motivations or editing time.

Reference:
(https://dailybruin.com/2007/04/15/ibets_editing_butchers_wire_story_linei/)

12.

The winner of the FIFA World Cup gets $38 million in prize money.

Reference:
(https://en.wikipedia.org/wiki/2018_FIFA_World_Cup#Prize_money)

13.

On August 3, 1914, a RFC pilot of an observation craft attacked a German pilot in midair, using all the ammo from his rifle, then his observer's pistol. He then threw the pistol at the German's propeller. This was the beginning of aviation warfare.

Reference: (http://www.eyewitnesstohistory.com/airwar1914.htm)

14.

After martial arts, parkour is booming amongst Iranian women, who are often seen practicing various jumps and rolls while still wearing the mandatory hijab.

Reference: (https://www.theguardian.com/lifeandstyle/the-womens-blog-with-jane-martinson/2013/jun/10/parkour-iranian-women-get-physical)

15.

Franklin D. Roosevelt and Teddy Roosevelt were fifth cousins, and Teddy was also Eleanor Roosevelt's uncle. Meaning that Franklin D. Roosevelt and Eleanor were married as fifth cousins once removed, and she never had to change her last name.

Reference: (https://www.history.com/this-day-in-history/franklin-roosevelt-marries-eleanor-roosevelt)

16.

Samoa never had a December 30, 2011, because they moved from the eastern side of the international dateline to the western side on December 29, therefore skipping a day. Employers were still required to pay their staff for December 30 even though it never existed.

Reference: (http://www.abc.net.au/news/2011-12-30/samoa-skips-friday-in-time-zone-change/3753350)

17.

Christine McVie of Fleetwood Mac wrote the song "You Make Loving Fun" about an affair she had with the band's lighting director. She told her husband, John McVie, that it was written about her dog, only for him to later find out what it was really about.

Reference: (https://en.wikipedia.org/wiki/You_Make_Loving_Fun)

18.

The tarantula hawk, a type of wasp that lives in the U.S., is said to have the most painful insect sting in the world.

Reference: (https://simple.wikipedia.org/wiki/Tarantula_hawk)

19.

Basketball player Charles Bassey was discovered in Nigeria by a coach at the age of 12 while selling fried chicken along the side of the road.

Reference: (https://en.wikipedia.org/wiki/Charles_Bassey)

20.

Studies of the Gebusi tribe in Papua New Guinea showed significant levels of male mortality due to the tribe deciding that an individual's behavior is so intolerable that for the good of the tribe they must be killed.

Reference: (https://theconversation.com/early-humans-had-to-become-more-feminine-before-they-could-dominate-the-planet-42952)

21.

Buzz Aldrin was the first person to have Communion in space.

Reference: (https://huffpost.com/us/entry/5600648)

22.

The kea bird, the world's only alpine parrot, was once hunted for bounty because it attacked sheep.

Reference: (https://en.wikipedia.org/wiki/Kea)

23.

Katee Sackhoff, formerly of "Battlestar Galactica," played Bitch Pudding on "Robot Chicken."

Reference: (https://www.youtube.com/watch?v=s3Y3lwCr66Q)

24.

Sweden has a naming law to separate non-noble families from having noble titles. In 1991, a couple attempted to name their child as "Brfxxccxxmnpcccclllmmnprxvclmnckssqlbb11116" to challenge the fine associated with it.

Reference:(https://en.wikipedia.org/wiki/Naming_law_in_Sweden#Brfxxccxxmnpcccclllmmnprxvclmnckssqlbb11116)

25.

After 300 years, the discovery of the Royal Arsenal of Nepal was found under a palace and recovered and sold to an antique arms dealer.

Reference: (https://www.youtube.com/watch?v=1yHOmgU4Afs)

26.

Castoreum from the beaver's scent glands is a natural source of acetylsalicylic acid, or aspirin.

Reference: (http://www.hbcheritage.ca/teacher-resources/TG-HBC-Beaver-ENG.pdf)

27.

The original Starbucks logo was perfectly symmetrical. However, people found it cold and lifeless so a small imperfection was added to make it look more human.

Reference: (https://www.adweek.com/creativity/how-a-hidden-design-flaw-makes-the-starbucks-logo-look-perfect/)

28.

The photosynthesizing Green Sea Slug is considered part animal and part plant.

Reference: (https://www.wired.com/2010/01/green-sea-slug/)

29.

The television show "Star Trek" aired 22 years before the first evidence of an exoplanet, in 1988, and 26 years before the first confirmed observation of an exoplanet.

Reference: (https://exoplanets.nasa.gov/news/1385/to-boldly-go-how-star-trek-inspired-nasas-planet-hunters/)

30.

The word for turkey in various languages has geographical connections. In English, there's turkey, in Turkish, it is called Hindi, a reference to India. French, Italian, Armenian and Hebrew also refer to it as an Indian bird, while Croatian, Hawaiian and Portuguese speakers call it Peru.

Reference:(http://www.slate.com/blogs/lexicon_valley/2014/11/25/turkey_in_turkish_and_other_geographically_implausible_names_for_this_bird.html)

31.

During Prohibition, federal agents Izzy Einstein and Moe Smith disguised themselves as grave-diggers, football players, Russian women, rabbis, judges, and plumbers. Together, they seized more than 5 million bottles of illicit booze and made 4,932 arrests.

Reference: (http://www.nydailynews.com/new-york/rumhounds-izzy-moe-turned-prohibition-arrests-comedy-article-1.787185)

32.

Bomb technicians make between $23,000 and $80,000.

Reference: (https://www.jobmonkey.com/uniquejobs2/bomb-jobs/)

33.

There's a theme park which offers children the experience of adulthood called KidZania. Instead of going on rides, kids can work in a variety of jobs, like fireman or pilot planes, and use their "salary" in the gift shop or rent electric versions of luxury cars.

Reference: (https://en.wikipedia.org/wiki/KidZania)

34.

People who binge watch TV shows report significantly less enjoyment than those who watch over the course of several days or weeks.

Reference:
(http://firstmonday.org/ojs/index.php/fm/article/view/7729/6532)

35.

The tiny Faroe Islands won their first-ever competitive international men's soccer match in 1990 against Austria in a game that had to be played in Sweden due to the country not having any grass soccer pitches at the time.

Reference: (http://outsideoftheboot.com/2016/04/26/faroe-islands-an-inspirational-story/)

36.

A kidney can be purchased for $650 in Kenya and sold for $200,000 in South Africa.

Reference: (https://www.havocscope.com/black-market-prices/organs-kidneys/)

37.

Suicide from overwork, Karojisatsu, and death from overwork, Karaoshi, are so prevalent in Japan that they have words for them.

Reference:
(http://www.ilo.org/safework/info/publications/WCMS_211571/lang--en/index.htm)

38.

Silent era comedian, Ben Turpin, believed that his crossed eyes were essential to his career; he would check the mirror if he received any blow to the head, and his friend would joke that they would pray for his eyes to be healed.

Reference: (https://en.wikipedia.org/wiki/Ben_Turpin)

39.

Chickens are omnivorous and will eat from grass to insects to large rodents, even each other if they get too hungry.

Reference: (https://www.westonaprice.org/health-topics/farm-ranch/chickens-are-omnivores-its-no-dilemma/)

40.

A Norwegian adventurer with a diverse group of people sailed from Morocco to Barbados using a boat made from Papyrus based on Ancient Egyptian models. He has also sailed from South America to Polynesian Islands using a raft.

Reference:
(https://en.wikipedia.org/wiki/Thor_Heyerdahl#Boats_Ra_and_Ra_II)

41.

Base metals like lead can be transmuted into gold using particle accelerators. The process is so expensive that it is not economically viable. Gold can also be turned into base metals.

Reference: (https://www.scientificamerican.com/article/fact-or-fiction-lead-can-be-turned-into-gold/)

42.

Tea was so important to wartime Britain, that in 1942, the government attempted to purchase all the tea in the world.

Reference: (https://blog.teabox.com/year-britain-bought-tea-world)

43.

Finnish people recycle over 90% of their cans and bottles. This is because they get part of their money back from the cost of the product.

Reference: (https://www.palpa.fi/beverage-container-recycling/deposit-refund-system/)

44.

Besides Chernobyl and Fukushima, there was a Soviet nuclear disaster that happened in 1957. The Kyshtym Disaster had a death toll that is estimated to be at 50 to more than 8,000. The CIA knew about it but covered it up to prevent panic affecting their own nuclear plants.

Reference: (https://www.britannica.com/event/Kyshtym-disaster)

45.

It costs more than double the amount of money per household to provide services to the suburbs than to a more urban area.

Reference: (https://usa.streetsblog.org/2015/03/05/sprawl-costs-the-public-more-than-twice-as-much-as-compact-development/)

46.

Patches of white hair are referred to as Poliosis and can be caused by genetic conditions, stress, and even taking certain medications. The localized depigmentation of hair is also known as a mallen streak or white forlock.

Reference: (https://en.wikipedia.org/wiki/Poliosis)

47.

Rob Zombie directed a commercial for Woolite.

Reference: (https://nerdist.com/rob-zombies-woolite-commercial/)

48.

Possum and opossum are not interchangeable terms. The possum in Australia is more closely related to the kangaroo.

Reference: (https://en.wikipedia.org/wiki/Opossum)

49.

John Solomon Rarey was a 19th century horse whisperer who tamed a horse named Cruiser which was known as "the fiercest horse ever seen". After meeting Rarey, Cruiser was said to be as gentle as a lamb. When Rarey died in 1866, Cruiser's bad temper returned.

Reference: (https://en.wikipedia.org/wiki/John_Solomon_Rarey)

50.

Bryan Adams' hit song "Run to You" was originally written by Adams and Jim Vallance for Blue Öyster Cult, but the group turned it down.

Reference:
(https://en.wikipedia.org/wiki/Run_to_You_(Bryan_Adams_song))

51.

Leo Hirschfield was an Austrian immigrant and avid inventor who first created the Tootsie products. He ended up being pushed out of "The Sweets Company of America" which was then selling his product, and took his own life in 1922, leaving a note which stated: "I'm sorry, but I couldn't help it."

Reference: (https://candyprofessor.com/2010/02/03/tootsie-roll-mystery/)

52.

One can perform the Heimlich Maneuver on oneself.

Reference: (https://medlineplus.gov/ency/imagepages/1100.htm)

53.

There's rather strong evidence that water in the Devil's Kettle waterfall simply rejoins the rest of the river shortly down its course.

Reference:
(https://en.wikipedia.org/wiki/Judge_C._R._Magney_State_Park#Devil's_Kettle)

54.

On January 1st, 2019, all works published in 1923 enter the public domain. This is the first public domain entrance of copyrighted material in 20 years.

Reference: (https://lifehacker.com/these-1923-copyrighted-works-enter-the-public-domain-in-1825241296)

55.

There were 12 American prisoners of war killed when the United States dropped "Little Boy" in Hiroshima.

Reference: (https://www.bostonmagazine.com/arts-entertainment/2016/05/27/remembering-american-soldiers-hiroshima/)

56.

New Zealand's first tank, the Bob Semple tank, was built from a tractor, sheet metal and 6 machine guns. When ridiculed for the design Bob Semple said, "I don't see anyone else coming up with any better ideas."

Reference: (https://en.wikipedia.org/wiki/Bob_Semple_tank)

57.

Scapegoating was an actual practice where a town would place all of their sins on to a goat and then cast it out of the town to die, thus "removing" the sin from the town's people.

Reference: (https://www.britannica.com/topic/scapegoat)

58.

Thomas Jefferson supported redistributing land in France from the rich to the poor, and was open to something similar being done in the U.S.

Reference: (http://press-pubs.uchicago.edu/founders/documents/v1ch15s32.html)

59.

Hubert Latham was the first to attempt to fly a plane over the English Channel in 1909; he failed, but in doing so he became the first person to ever land a plane on water.

Reference: (https://en.wikipedia.org/wiki/Hubert_Latham)

60.

Phytophotodermatitis is a skin condition caused by exposure to sunlight after handling citrus fruits.

Reference: (https://en.wikipedia.org/wiki/Phytophotodermatitis)

61.

The Knights of Malta is a sovereign entity, part of the U.N. General Assembly, with 13,500 knights, 40,000 doctors and a further 80,000 volunteers. They have only 2 official citizens, but they still issue passports, coins and postage stamps despite having no physical land or territory.

Reference:
(https://wikipedia.org/wiki/Sovereign_Military_Order_of_Malta)

62.

The Thrawn trilogy by Timothy Zahn is credited with helping to revitalize the Star Wars franchise in 1991 with the release of the first novel in the trilogy, Heir to the Empire, and formalizing the Star Wars Expanded Universe.

Reference: (https://www.starwars.com/news/heir-to-the-empire-critical-reaction)

63.

There is a permanent gold postbox in each of the home towns of 2012 British Gold Medal winners.

Reference:(https://en.wikipedia.org/wiki/2012_Summer_Olympics_and_Paralympics_gold_post_boxes)

64.

Pandas will sometimes fake pregnancies to receive more food and special treatment from humans.

Reference: (https://edition.cnn.com/2014/08/27/world/asia/china-panda-pregnancy/index.html?no-st=9999999999)

65.

A native tribe in California had a game just like soccer, where players kicked the ball through goals on a 100-meter field. Men and women played together, men had to kick the ball, but women could use their hands.

Reference: (http://www.parks.ca.gov/?page_id=935)

66.

Moscow has many underground sites like bomb shelters or a speculated secret Metro system, parallel to the public one, used by the Russian Military and maybe an underground city as well.

Reference: (https://www.inyourpocket.com/moscow/the-city-beneath-the-city_74522f)

67.

South Koreans have grown 3 inches taller than their North Koreans counterparts. They are genetically the same and have been living similar lives until the divide in the last century. The nutritional difference of only 50 to 60 years has caused this difference.

Reference: (https://www.bbc.com/news/magazine-17774210)

68.

1 gram of antimatter costs approximately 62 trillion dollars.

Reference: (https://science.nasa.gov/science-news/science-at-nasa/1999/prop12apr99_1)

69.

Norwegian police banned a team of Finnish divers from a cave in 2014 after 2 people died. In secret, the divers pulled their 2 dead friends to the surface and fulfilled a promise to a widow of one man. The illegal rescue took 27 divers and 101 hours in frigid water, using about 1-ton of equipment.

Reference: (https://www.bbc.com/news/magazine-36097300)

70.

Our DNA changes constantly over the course of our lifetime.

Reference: (https://genetics.thetech.org/original_news/news91)

71.

Cherry pits contain amygdalin, which can produce cyanide when metabolized.

Reference: (https://www.bonappetit.com/test-kitchen/ingredients/slideshow/foods-that-can-kill-you)

72.

The ConIFA World Cup is a football tournament for countries not recognized as official by FIFA. Competitors include Tibet, North Cyprus, and West Armenia.

Reference: (https://en.wikipedia.org/wiki/2018_ConIFA_World_Football_Cup)

73.

The bends was originally known as "caisson disease". Construction workers in pressurized caissons would immediately come out into normal pressure and get sick.

Reference: (https://www.ncbi.nlm.nih.gov/pubmed/15686275)

74.

Babe Ruth was only captain of the New York Yankees for 5 days early in his tenure with the team. He was fired for trying to attack a heckler in the stands, which made the front page of the New York Times.

Reference: (https://timesmachine.nytimes.com/timesmachine/1922/05/27/109840912.pdf)

75.

Park rangers in South Africa are removing rhino's horns, so poachers won't kill the rhinos for their horns.

Reference: (https://youtu.be/UugTT0ReJCM)

76.

Hysterical blindness is now generally referred to as conversion disorder. This disorder occurs in people who go blind or paralyzed as the result of trauma or a high level of stress.

Reference: (https://en.wikipedia.org/wiki/Conversion_disorder)

77.

Cats and dogs drink water by using the backs of their tongue to create a ladle.

Reference: (https://antranik.org/the-ingenious-way-cats-and-dogs-drink-water/)

78.

Skiing enthusiasts on Usenet got into a flame war that went on for months until the Seattle police department had to intervene, and a judge banned one of the members from making any new posts. The dispute began over who should get a set of free ski-lift passes.

Reference: (https://www.wired.com/1999/11/usenet-ban-a-slippery-slope/)

79.

On no less than three separate occasions, children have been served alcohol instead of apple juice at Applebee's restaurants.

Reference: (https://abcnews.go.com/amp/US/detroit-applebees-mistakenly-serves-alcohol-child/story?id=13345868)

80.

The acid mantle is a thin, slightly acidic film on human skin acting as a barrier to protect the skin from bacteria, viruses and contaminates.

Reference: (https://en.wikipedia.org/wiki/Acid_mantle)

81.

The reason children get lice but adults rarely do is because your scalp gets more acidic after puberty.

Reference: (https://headlicecenter.com/how-do-you-get-head-lice-children-more-often-than-adults/)

82.

A lepidopterist is a person who studies or collects butterflies and moths.

Reference: (https://en.wikipedia.org/wiki/Lepidopterology)

83.

Famous aviator Charles Lindbergh toured the Pacific during World War II as a "civilian observer." During this time, he flew some 50 combat missions in Corsairs and P-38s, figured out techniques to increase the range of both planes, and shot down a Japanese plane.

Reference:
(https://en.wikipedia.org/wiki/Charles_Lindbergh#World_War_II)

84.

In severe hypothermia, people strip off all their clothes, dig a hole, and die in it.

Reference: (https://www.ncbi.nlm.nih.gov/pubmed/7632602)

85.

London 2012 organizers approached the band manager of The Who to ask if Keith Moon could play at the Olympics ceremony. Keith Moon passed away in 1978.

Reference: (https://www.theguardian.com/music/us-news-blog/2012/apr/13/keith-moon-london-olympics-organisers)

86.

For Disney's "Tangled", the company had to hire Kelly Ward, who has a Ph.D. in animating human hair, to help with the simulation and physics of Rapunzel's locks. That hair also weighs 60 to 80 pounds and is about 70 feet long.

Reference: (http://www.gpb.org/blogs/passion-for-learning/2012/06/06/disneys-tangled-an-exercise-in-physics-and-computer-animation)

87.

In 2003, a kid hacked into Valve and stole the Half Life 2 source code.

Reference: (https://www.eurogamer.net/articles/2011-02-21-the-boy-who-stole-half-life-2-article)

88.

Alessandro Zarrelli, in 2004, conned 22 football clubs across the U.K. into thinking he was one of Italy's best young prospects by impersonating a non-existent executive at the Italian Football Federation and writing letters offering his services.

Reference: (https://en.wikipedia.org/wiki/Alessandro_Zarrelli)

89.

Artist Yayoi Kusama, currently exhibiting her "Infinity Mirrors", has been voluntarily committed to a sanatorium since the late 1970s, only leaving to paint in the building across the street.

Reference: (http://observer.com/2015/04/the-stunning-story-of-the-woman-who-is-the-worlds-most-popular-artist/)

90.

During the 1930's and 1940's, the Japanese secret service sold opium and heroin infused cigarettes to China in order to get them hooked.

Reference:(https://en.wikipedia.org/wiki/Golden_Bat_(cigarette)#Opium_in_Chinese_sold_Golden_Bat_cigarettes)

91.

The people of North Sentinel Island, often described as uncontacted, were visited extensively in the 1990s. They hunt wild pig, their songs contain two notes, and their only form of art is body painting. Researchers compare them to humans 15,000 years ago.

Reference: (https://www.independent.co.uk/news/world/islanders-running-out-of-isolation-tim-mcgirk-in-the-andaman-islands-reports-on-the-fate-of-the-1477566.html)

92.

The originator of Mr. Hands, from the Mr. Bill short films, is Vance DeGeneres, Ellen DeGenerges' brother.

Reference: (https://en.wikipedia.org/wiki/Vance_DeGeneres)

93.

The world's largest axe, which is over 50 feet long with a blade of over 30 feet, is located in New Brunswick, Canada.

Reference:
(https://www.tourismnewbrunswick.ca/Products/W/Worlds-Largest-Axe.aspx)

94.

A boy was struck by lightning at the foot of a roller coaster called "Zeus' Thunder".

Reference:
(https://en.wikipedia.org/wiki/Parc_Ast%C3%A9rix#Incidents)

95.

Between 63rd and 76th streets in New York City, scientists discovered an ant species found nowhere else on Earth. It has been nicknamed the "ManhattAnt."

Reference: (https://www.smithsonianmag.com/smart-news/nyc-has-its-own-ant-the-manhattant-25741340/)

96.

In the 1960s, a group of Australian patrolmen encountered a group of Indigenous Australians who had no contact with Europeans while evacuating a dump area for an experimental rocket.

Reference:
(https://www.youtube.com/watch?v=nWuOeBYjek0&t=1890s)

97.

The word "materiel" refers to military objects, equipment and hardware, and is not the word "material" misspelled.

Reference: (https://en.wikipedia.org/wiki/Materiel)

98.

A Hungarian company strapped two MIG fighter jet engines to a Soviet era tank and used it to put out oil well fires.

Reference: (https://www.caranddriver.com/features/stilling-the-fires-of-war-big-wind-page-2)

99.

Germany won 2 gold medals in the Olympics for Town Planning.

Reference:(https://en.wikipedia.org/wiki/List_of_Olympic_medalists_in_art_competitions#Town_planning)

100.

The dictator of Turkmenistan, Saparmurat Niyazov, banned news reporters and anchors from wearing make-up on television, because he said he found it difficult to distinguish male anchors from female anchors.

Reference: (https://en.wikipedia.org/wiki/Saparmurat_Niyazov)

101.

During the Banana Massacre of 1928, the U.S. threatened Colombia with military invasion if it didn't end the ongoing Chiquita workers' strike. The Colombian army fired on unarmed protesters, men, women, and children, killing somewhere between 800 and 3,000.

Reference: (https://en.wikipedia.org/wiki/Banana_massacre)

102.

Richard Petty let a U.K. reporter ride around in the 1970 #43 Plymouth Superbird.

Reference:
(https://www.youtube.com/watch?v=C9LFgsLQATc&t=393)

103.

A case involving the use of the phrase "bong hits for Jesus" has been brought before the Supreme Court.

Reference: (https://www.oyez.org/cases/2006/06-278)

104.

The Outer Banks off of North Carolina stretches for 200 miles but its maximum width is only 3 miles, with most of the island being much smaller.

Reference: (http://www.outerbanksofnc.org/)

105.

There is a 3000-year old Chinese tradition called Ghost Marriages, or the marriage of two people who died single. In some cases, the parents of unmarried men buy female corpses so their sons could have a wife in afterlife.

Reference: (http://www.abc.net.au/news/2018-04-07/ghost-marriages-in-rural-china-continue-to-thrive/9608624)

106.

The winner of the marathon in the first modern day Olympics, held in 1896, stopped during the race for a glass of wine.

Reference: (https://vinepair.com/wine-blog/spyridon-louis-1896-olympics-marathon-wine/)

107.

Gustave Eiffel was the lead architect of the Statue of Liberty from 1880 to 1883. Four years later, he began building the Eiffel Tower.

Reference: (https://www.nps.gov/stli/learn/historyculture/alexandre-gustave-eiffel.htm)

108.

The early usage of the word "fuck" is from English court-records in 1310. The records mention a man named "Roger Fuckbythenavele". It is believed that Roger was a man who had tried, through ignorance, to have sexual intercourse through his partner's navel.

Reference: (https://en.wikipedia.org/wiki/Roger_Fuckebythenavele)

109.

There was an engine that put out only 600HP, but at 39,000 feet per pound of torque.

Reference: (https://www.youtube.com/watch?v=HzFzpH-sDjs)

110.

On "Full House Bob Saget," John Stamos and Dave Coulier often got in trouble for "adult humor" in front of their child co-stars and got busted doing whip its off screen with 15 cans of Redi Whip while impatiently waiting for the girls to finish shooting a scene.

Reference: (https://screenrant.com/full-house-dark-secrets-behind-the-scenes/)

111.

U.S. Soccer Player Christian Pulisic has dual U.S. and Croatian citizenship, and turned down a spot on Croatia's National Team two years ago to instead play for the U.S.

Reference: (https://en.wikipedia.org/wiki/Christian_Pulisic)

112.

The Belgian version of "Dragostea Din Tei", or "Numa Numa", is about following traffic laws.

Reference: (https://www.youtube.com/watch?v=zvwgU3az1_g)

113.

A logo for the 2012 Olympics parodying internet shock site Goatse.cx was unknowingly chosen by BBC.co.uk site keepers as one of the 12 best user-submitted logos for the event.

Reference:
(https://www.theregister.co.uk/2007/06/04/bbc_olympics_cx/)

114.

The island nation of Mauritius is the only African country in which the majority religion is Hinduism.

Reference: (https://en.wikipedia.org/wiki/Mauritius#Religion)

115.

"Pretty Woman's" original ending, Vivian doesn't ride off with Edward. Instead, she gets on a bus with Kitt anticipating a fun day financed by Vivian's week with Edward, as Vivian, "stares out emptily ahead."

Reference: (https://www.vanityfair.com/hollywood/2015/03/pretty-woman-original-ending/amp)

116.

A 10 year old girl from the U.S. wrote a letter to Soviet leader Andropov concerning nuclear holocaust. She was then invited by him and went to the USSR. She died 2 years after her return in a plane crash.

Reference: (https://en.wikipedia.org/wiki/Samantha_Smith)

117.

Military computers built in the 1950s were reused as TV show and movie props as recently as the 1996 "Independence Day" movie and the 2010 "The Event."

Reference: (https://en.wikipedia.org/wiki/AN/FSQ-7_Combat_Direction_Central)

118.

Operating for over 1,400 years, Kongō Gumi, a construction company in Japan, is the oldest continuously ongoing independent company.

Reference: (https://en.wikipedia.org/wiki/Kong%C5%8D_Gumi)

119.

In 2001, NASA launched Mars Odyssey to Mars.

Reference: (https://www.space.com/13558-historic-mars-missions.html)

120.

The Babylonians created the 7 day week because there are 7 celestial bodies visible to the naked eye.

Reference: (https://www.scienceabc.com/eyeopeners/why-do-we-have-seven-days-in-a-week.html)

121.

"The Rolling Stone" played with 1 big inflatable penis on the stage during the "Tour of the Americas" in 1975.

Reference: (https://ohfact.com/interesting-facts-about-rolling-stones/)

122.

The first pair of soccer cleats were made for King Henry VIII in the 1500's.

Reference: (http://www.soccer365.com/short-history-of-the-soccer-cleat/)

123.

Chess boxing is a game in which competitors fight in alternating rounds of chess and boxing. This real competitive sport has 11 rounds and is won when an opponent is knocked out while boxing or is defeated in chess.

Reference: (https://en.wikipedia.org/wiki/Chess_boxing)

124.

A baby can be born with the DNA of 3 parents.

Reference: (https://www.cbsnews.com/news/first-3-parent-dna-baby-born-rare-disease/)

125.

The animal with the fastest wingbeat is the midge, with 62,760 beats per minute.

Reference: (https://www.si.edu/spotlight/buginfo/insect-flight)

126.

Freddie Mercury of Queen, was not from England, but in fact, was African and from Tanzania.

Reference: (https://www.biography.com/people/freddie-mercury-9406228)

127.

The "burgh" at the end of "Pittsburgh" was originally pronounced the same way as in "Edinburgh" but changed during the 1800's due to influence from the German word "burg". In 1890, the name was even officially changed to "Pittsburg", but was later changed back.

Reference: (https://en.wikipedia.org/wiki/Name_of_Pittsburgh)

128.

In 1966, the FIFA World Cup trophy was stolen off England, only to be found 7 days later in a garden by a dog named Pickles.

Reference:(http://news.bbc.co.uk/onthisday/hi/dates/stories/march/20/newsid_2861000/2861545.stm)

129.

Elephant Butte is a summit in New Mexico that got its name from its shape, said to look like an elephant. In 2014, campers on the summit stumbled upon a fossil of a Stegomastodon, the prehistoric ancestor of the elephant.

Reference:
(https://en.wikipedia.org/wiki/Elephant_Butte_(Sierra_County,_New_Mexico))

130.

The founder of the Thule Society, a group in Germany that sponsored the German Workers' Party, a political party that Hitler would join and transform into the Nazi Party, converted to Islam.

Reference: (https://en.wikipedia.org/wiki/Rudolf_von_Sebottendorf)

131.

The founder of Beavertown Brewery is the son of Robert Plant, the Led Zeppelin front man.

Reference: (https://www.theguardian.com/small-business-network/2017/jun/13/logan-plant-beavertown-led-zeppelin-robert-plant-beer)

132.

Baseball Hall of Fame pitcher Rube Waddell would often be distracted by shiny things, puppies, and balloons while on the mound. He once ran off the field to chase a fire truck on the way to a fire.

Reference: (http://fromdeeprightfield.com/rube-waddell-the-first-american-league-ace)

133.

Joyce Vincent was a British woman who died in her home. Her death went unnoticed for over two years until her house was repossessed.

Reference: (https://en.wikipedia.org/wiki/Joyce_Vincent)

134.

Stevie Nicks was asked to compose and perform a song for the "American Gigolo" soundtrack, but her contract with Modern Records prevented her from doing so. Debbie Harry was approached next, and the resulting song was Blondie's #1 hit, "Call Me".

Reference: (https://en.wikipedia.org/wiki/Call_Me_(Blondie_song))

135.

Plants share nutrients and data through a massive underground fungal network.

Reference: (http://www.bbc.com/earth/story/20141111-plants-have-a-hidden-internet?oid=fbert)

136.

We're all at least 50th cousins to everyone else on Earth today.

Reference: (https://io9.gizmodo.com/5791530/why-humans-all-much-more-related-than-you-think)

137.

The Wait Calculation is a dilemma stating that during the millennia long trip to another star system, humanity would easily find ways to increase travel speed greatly, meaning any new expeditions would arrive much earlier. Therefore, no-one would risk wasting their lives on such a meaningless trip.

Reference:(https://ipfs.io/ipfs/QmXoypizjW3WknFiJnKLwHCnL72vedxjQkDDP1mXWo6uco/wiki/Wait_Calculation.html)

138.

In 1950, Brazil were so sure they would win the FIFA World Cup final against Uruguay that the local media hailed them as "future champions" before the match and 22 gold medals had already been made with the names of Brazilian players. They lost 2-1.

Reference:
(https://en.wikipedia.org/wiki/Uruguay_v_Brazil_(1950_FIFA_Worl
d_Cup))

139.

The Fukushima event was placed in the same class as the Chernobyl disaster on the International Nuclear and Radiological event scale.

Reference: (https://www.bbc.com/news/science-environment-
13048916)

140.

Heinz ketchup can't legally be called "ketchup" in Israel because it doesn't contain enough tomato paste.

Reference: (https://mashable.com/2015/08/24/heinz-kechup-
israel/#uTsVCtKxlaqX)

141.

The phone area code for Brevard County, Florida, is 321 in reference to the rockets launches that are conducted there.

Reference: (http://brevard.happeningmag.com/why-we-heart-
brevard-reason-2-area-code-321)

142.

The jewel wasp injects a special chemical blend into the brains of cockroaches, making them pawns in the jewel wasp's control and perfect live food for its offspring.

Reference: (https://www.scientificamerican.com/article/how-a-wasp-
turns-cockroaches-into-zombies/)

143.

Lindsay Lohan attempted to sue Rockstar Games stating the character Lacey Jones in Grand Theft Auto 5 was based on her.

Reference: (https://www.bbc.co.uk/news/technology-43596000)

144.

During the Green Corn Rebellion, White, Native, Tenant and African American farmers rebelled against the U.S. government to enforce the Selective Draft Act of 1917. Afterwards, only 3 died but hundreds of Socialists and IWW were arrested and discredited.

Reference: (https://en.wikipedia.org/wiki/Green_Corn_Rebellion)

145.

During the Great Eel Riot of 1886, a massive riot in Amsterdam left 26 dead and countless injured, all over a law banning the popular sport of "eel pulling".

Reference: (http://www.24oranges.nl/2016/09/11/the-eel-riots-of-1886-ended-with-26-people-and-1-eel-dead/)

146.

The largest take of sperm whales occurred not in the 1800s, but the 1960s.

Reference:
(https://en.wikipedia.org/wiki/Sperm_whaling#20th_century)

147.

Fungus is more closely related to animals than plants.

Reference: (https://en.wikipedia.org/wiki/Fungus)

148.

The Great Whiskey Fire of Dublin killed 13 people in 1875. No one perished as a result of smoke inhalation or burns. All victims died of alcohol poisoning by drinking the whiskey flowing through the streets.

Reference: (https://www.irishtimes.com/news/offbeat/the-night-a-river-of-whiskey-ran-through-the-streets-of-dublin-1.2743517)

149.

The first Paddington Bear stuffed toy to be manufactured was created in 1972 by Gabrielle Designs, a small business run by Shirley and Eddie Clarkson, with the prototype made as a Christmas present for their children Joanna and Jeremy Clarkson.

Reference: (https://en.wikipedia.org/wiki/Paddington_Bear)

150.

Morrissey won an award in 2015 for Worst Sex Scene in his novel "List of the Lost".

Reference: (https://news.avclub.com/morrissey-wins-award-for-worst-literary-sex-scene-1798286893)

151.

"Knocker-uppers" was a profession with the sole purpose of waking people up in the morning, later to become obsolete by alarm clocks.

Reference: (https://www.bbc.com/news/uk-england-35840393)

152.

The global population has grown 145 percent since 1960, incomes have grown by 183 percent over the same period.

Reference: (https://humanprogress.org/article.php?p=1180)

153.

Penicillin was discovered accidentally after scientist Alexander Fleming left a window open allowing mold to grow on a contaminated Petri dish.

Reference: (https://www.healio.com/endocrinology/news/print/endocrine-today/%7B15afd2a1-2084-4ca6-a4e6-7185f5c4cfb0%7D/penicillin-an-accidental-discovery-changed-the-course-of-medicine)

154.

The richest preacher in the world is David Oyedepo of Nigeria, with a net worth of $150 million. The 63-year old pastor owns 2 private jets, a $10 million house, and controls churches in 45 African nations.

Reference: (http://www.informationng.com/2018/01/bishop-david-oyedepo-tops-forbes-list-richest-pastors-world-net-worth-150m.html)

155.

TV Chicken got its name from the fact that the customers can watch their chicken being roasted in an oven with a glass window.

Reference: (https://www.atlasobscura.com/foods/tv-chicken-uganda)

156.

Modern gunpowder contains its own oxidizer for combustion, meaning you could fire a gun in space.

Reference: (https://amp-livescience-com.cdn.ampproject.org/v/s/amp.livescience.com/18588-shoot-gun-space.html?usqp=mq331AQECAE4AQ%3D%3D&_js_v=0.1#referrer=https://www.google.com&_tf=From%20%251%24s)

157.

There is a black market for sand.

Reference: (https://www.nytimes.com/2016/06/23/opinion/the-worlds-disappearing-sand.html)

158.

Ocho de Plata, the Spanish Dollar, was the first legal tender in the United States until the Coinage Act of 1857. In fact, equity shares were still quoted in eighths of a dollar until 2001; this was a legacy from the coin's divisibility by 8, since each Spanish Dollar was worth 8 reales.

Reference: (https://en.wikipedia.org/wiki/Spanish_dollar)

159.

There are approximately 100,000 active phone booths still left in the U.S.

Reference: (https://slashdot.org/story/18/03/20/2040212/there-are-still-100000-pay-phones-in-the-us)

160.

"Arsenic Eaters" were a group of Austrians who ingested doses far beyond the lethal dose of arsenic trioxide without any apparent harm. They used to eat up small doses initially and gradually built up to 300 to 400 milligrams as a mithridate to help enable strenuous work at high altitudes in the Alps.

Reference: (https://www.nytimes.com/1885/07/26/archives/arsenic-eaters.html)

161.

Frisland was a "phantom" island off the coast of Greenland which, despite being nonexistent, was charted on nearly every map of the North Atlantic from the 1560s to the 1660s.

Reference: (https://en.wikipedia.org/wiki/Frisland)

162.

Many French Bulldogs require artificial insemination to breed because their hips are too slim to allow the male to mount the female. In addition, 80% of their litters are delivered through C-section.

Reference:
(https://en.wikipedia.org/wiki/French_Bulldog#Birth_and_reproduction)

163.

After surviving the explosion of a rocket launch failure, the first thing the Soviet cosmonauts asked their rescue crews was cigarettes, but they were given shots of vodka instead.

Reference: (https://en.wikipedia.org/wiki/Soyuz_7K-ST_No._16L)

164.

Human blood boils at approximately the same temperature as water, 100 degrees Celsius.

Reference: (http://www.madsci.org/posts/archives/2003-09/1062886605.Bc.r.html)

165.

The Vulcan Salute from "Star Trek" was actually based off of an ancient Jewish hand sign used in the priestly blessing. Leonard Nimoy, a Jewish man, based the iconic gesture off the age old Jewish tradition.

Reference: (https://en.wikipedia.org/wiki/Vulcan_salute)

166.

Elvis Presley allied himself with FBI director Edgar Hoover and encouraged him to have John Lennon thrown out of the U.S.

Reference:
(https://www.filmibeat.com/music/international/2011/jones-presley-wanted-beatup-lennon-070111.html)

167.

Legally speaking, there is only a single town in Pennsylvania; Bloomsburg. Every other municipality is either a city, township, or borough.

Reference:
(https://en.wikipedia.org/wiki/List_of_municipalities_in_Pennsylvania)

168.

Dwayne Johnson has been in almost 40 movies since 1999.

Reference:
(https://en.wikipedia.org/wiki/Dwayne_Johnson_filmography)

169.

Eyewitness misidentification is the greatest contributing factor to wrongful convictions proven by DNA testing, playing a role in more than 70% of convictions overturned through DNA testing nationwide.

Reference: (https://www.innocenceproject.org/causes/eyewitness-misidentification/)

170.

The J-SH04 was a mobile phone made by Sharp Corporation and released by J-Phone. It was only available in Japan, and was released in November 2000. It was Japan's first ever phone with a built-in camera and color display.

Reference: (https://en.wikipedia.org/wiki/J-SH04)

171.

The McDonald's golden arches in Sedona, Arizona, were made turquoise when the yellow color had been deemed by government officials to be contrasting too much against the scenic red rock.

Reference: (https://www.aol.com/article/2014/09/02/turquoise-mcdonalds-arches-ordered-in-arizona-town/20955898/)

172.

In the 1964 production of "Rudolph the Red Nosed Reindeer", the Roman Numeral in the opening credits that was meant to be 1964 was instead accidentally made 1164.

Reference: (https://www.moviemistakes.com/entry107372)

173.

Chimney sweeps' carcinoma was a deadly cancer of the scrotum that affected chimney sweeps, as young as 8 years old; one treatment was to cut it off without anesthesia and another was an arsenic paste.

Reference:
(https://en.wikipedia.org/wiki/Chimney_sweeps%27_carcinoma)

174.

In the nation of Papua New Guinea there are 820 different spoken languages, which belong to 60 language families as different from each other as French and Chinese.

Reference:(http://dwu.ac.pg/en/images/Research_Journal/2005/7%20Levy%20Language%20Research%20in%20PNG%2079-92.pdf)

175.

After the 1966 FIFA World Cup final, many newspapers referred to the "Russian linesman" who awarded the goal, as Azerbaijan was part of the Soviet Union at the time, and the nickname stuck to the point where his real name was all but forgotten.

Reference: (https://en.wikipedia.org/wiki/Tofiq_Bahramov)

176.

Superman and Kryptonite were selected to be named two genes in Arabidopsis thaliana. The former controls the flower development, while the latter silences the Superman gene.

Reference: (https://www.ncbi.nlm.nih.gov/pubmed/11898023)

177.

George Lucas wanted David Lynch to direct "Return of the Jedi."

Reference: (https://movieweb.com/return-of-the-jedi-david-lynch-director-twin-peaks/)

178.

In the "chicken poop prison" in Thailand, the ceiling of the cells was a grate, and chickens were cared for above the cell. Their dung was then allowed to drop freely onto the criminal within.

Reference: (https://www.bangkokpost.com/travel/sightseeing/5535/khuk-khi-kai)

179.

You are not supposed to take your dogs on an escalator as it can cause them serious injury.

Reference: (https://www.consumeraffairs.com/news/escalators-are-no-place-for-a-dog-082114.html)

180.

Electromagnetic waves or light can only be created via energy losses to electrons or the nucleus.

Reference: (http://sphericalhysterical.com/physics/ray-wave-optics/)

181.

The "Suspension Bridge Effect" and the Misattribution of Arousal are the same thing.

Reference: (https://en.wikipedia.org/wiki/Misattribution_of_arousal)

182.

Capybaras, the world's largest rodent, have been used as Seeing Eye animals.

Reference: (https://www.zmescience.com/other/feature-post/animal-files-capybaras-worlds-largest-rodents/)

183.

The theme of Eyewitness News was taken from Cool Hand Luke.

Reference:
(https://en.wikipedia.org/wiki/Eyewitness_News#Music_package)

184.

The Seinfeld episode "The Revenge" was based on the true story of Larry David quitting his Saturday Night Live writing gig.

Reference: (https://www.vanityfair.com/news/2017/10/larry-david-re-enacts-how-he-quit-saturday-night-live)

185.

In Houston, a family of 8 lived in a storage unit for 5 years.

Reference: (https://abcnews.go.com/Business/houston-texas-family-living-storage-shed/story?id=14009261)

186.

NASA's Kessler Telescope used the power of solar rays to replace a malfunctioning part.

Reference: (https://www.theverge.com/2014/12/30/7424343/nasa-kepler-telescope-rescue-mission-search-for-planets)

187.

Kitzmiller v. Dover Area School District, was the first direct challenge brought in the United States federal courts testing a public school district policy that required the teaching of intelligent design. The Dover Area School District lost paying $1,000,011 in legal fees.

Reference: (https://en.wikipedia.org/wiki/Kitzmiller_v._Dover_Area_School_District)

188.

The terms "grandstanding", "rain check", and "in one's wheelhouse" all come from baseball lingo.

Reference: (https://en.wikipedia.org/wiki/Glossary_of_English-language_idioms_derived_from_baseball)

189.

Bagel-Heading is a type of body modification pioneered in Canada and practiced in the Japanese underground scene. It is a temporary swelling distortion of the forehead created by a saline drip and often shaped to resemble a bagel or doughnut.

Reference: (https://en.wikipedia.org/wiki/Bagel_head)

190.

Upon learning of Johan Cruyff's transfer after 17 seasons to FC Barcelona in 1973, Ajax Amsterdam swapped his mother to a seat in the stadium behind a pole. For many years, she had been the cleaner of the club dressing rooms, and it was also where, as a widow, she had met her second husband.

Reference:
(https://en.wikiquote.org/wiki/Johan_Cruyff#Quotes_of_Cruyff)

191.

In Detroit, you can head south and get to Canada.

Reference: (http://www.howderfamily.com/blog/south-of-detroit/)

192.

Progressive creationism is the religious belief that God created new forms of life gradually over a period of hundreds of millions of years. In this view, creation occurred in rapid bursts in which all "kinds" of plants and animals appear in stages lasting millions of years.

Reference: (https://en.wikipedia.org/wiki/Progressive_creationism)

193.

The U.S. FDA has consistently identified antibiotic resistant bacteria in supermarket meat.

Reference:
(https://www.fda.gov/AnimalVeterinary/NewsEvents/CVMUpdates/ucm581433.htm)

194.

Liquid cremation is an alternative to using flame to cremate the body's liquid chemicals.

Reference: (https://gizmodo.com/what-is-liquid-cremation-and-why-is-it-illegal-1696897615)

195.

A manual found in an Aum facility contained the lyrics for a song entitled "Song of Sarin, the Magician."

Reference: (https://fas.org/irp/congress/1995_rpt/aum/part04.htm)

196.

Rapper Nelly missed out on a potential bone marrow donor for his dying sister who had leukemia because people protested his fundraiser due to his music video "Tip Drill."

Reference: (https://madamenoire.com/322872/nellys-still-mad-spelmans-tip-drill-protestand-good-reason/)

197.

Since 1993, McDonald's has had a dedicated delivery fleet on motorcycles in many Latin American countries.

Reference: (https://en.wikipedia.org/wiki/McDelivery)

198.

The reason The Mother Bird in Disney's "Alice in Wonderland" calls her a serpent is because in the novel her neck grows long, reaching up to the trees. In the film, they simply made her gigantic, but left this dialogue in anyway, thus rendering the serpent-reference pure nonsense.

Reference: (http://www.alice-in-wonderland.net/resources/analysis/interpretive-essays/alices-adventures-in-algebra/)

199.

In the first draft of the critically acclaimed "Star Trek: The Next Generation" episode "The Inner Light", an advertising blimp causes Picard to experience being on an island in a love triangle with Riker and Ensign Ro Laren.

Reference: (https://io9.gizmodo.com/the-making-of-star-trek-the-next-generations-greatest-1786330645)

200.

Many ships engaged in illegal, unreported and unregulated fishing often fly the flag of Mongolia. Being a land-locked country, Mongolia is one of the Flag of Convenience nations and has weak or no fishing regulations.

Reference: (http://globalfishingwatch.org/fisheries/flag-of-convenience-or-cloak-of-malfeasance/)

201.

A Royal Air Force soldier Nicholas Stephen Alkemade reportedly fell 18,000 feet without a parachute and survived.

Reference: (https://en.wikipedia.org/wiki/Nicholas_Alkemade)

202.

The real color of our Sun is white, not yellow.

Reference: (https://www.universetoday.com/18689/color-of-the-sun/)

203.

Jellyfish reproduce sexually and asexually. When sexual, the younglings plant themselves and grow to resemble sea plants.

Reference: (https://ocean.si.edu/ocean-life/invertebrates/jellyfish-and-comb-jellies#section_16508)

204.

The "division symbol" is actually named the "Obelus", and the ISO standard for mathematical signs says that it "should not be used" for division.

Reference: (https://en.wikipedia.org/wiki/Obelus)

205.

Chic, the band, have been nominated eleven times for the Rock and Roll Hall of Fame but never inducted.

Reference: (http://www.futurerocklegends.com/The_Snub_List.php)

206.

Geckos don't have eyelids. They clean their eyeballs by quickly licking it.

Reference: (https://www.youtube.com/watch?v=EUyOGTJszWA)

207.

Steve Hartman is credited as the inventor of the pool noodle, but Rick Koster insists he is. This disagreement stretches back to the 1980s.

Reference: (https://www.pressreader.com/canada/starmetro-toronto/20140627/281487864439171)

208.

In certain cases of kidnappings or hostage-taking, the victim develops feelings of trust or affection towards their captor. This is known as Stockholm syndrome.

Reference: (https://www.britannica.com/science/Stockholm-syndrome)

209.

The hooks and bass lines for the 1983 Yes hit "Owner of a Lonely Heart" were worked out by guitarist Trevor Rabin while he was on the toilet.

Reference: (https://en.wikipedia.org/wiki/90125#Songs)

210.

There are more molecules of air in a breath of air that you take than there are breaths of air in all the world's atmosphere.

Reference: (http://www.physics-astronomy.com/2014/04/the-18-best-neil-degrasse-tyson-quotes.html?m=1#.Wz_EYJ9OmdM)

211.

Modern ads are often digitally put in to syndicated re-runs of old shows like Friends and How I Met Your Mother.

Reference: (http://adage.com/article/madisonvine-people-players/inside-digitially-inserted-product-placement-business/48138/)

212.

The infamous BO-like smell of Limburger cheese is equally as effective at attracting mosquitos as the smell of a human foot, according to a peer-tested medical review.

Reference: (https://en.wikipedia.org/wiki/Limburger#Uses)

213.

In World War II, the British deployed 100,000 weather balloons trailing metal wires in order to short circuit and damage German power lines. The operation was deemed a success.

Reference: (https://en.wikipedia.org/wiki/Operation_Outward)

214.

Survivor generated controversy when, for its 13th season, the decision was made to divide the contestants into four tribes based on ethnicity.

Reference: (https://en.wikipedia.org/wiki/Survivor:_Cook_Islands)

215.

The towns of Liberal, Kansas, and Olney, U.K., compete in an annual pancake race. The competitors must wear an apron, cap, and pancake in order to compete.

Reference: (http://www.visitolney.com/Pancake-Race)

216.

Evangeline Lilly did an ad for Live Links before she was on "Lost."

Reference:
(https://www.youtube.com/watch?v=dlCzZLHtYds&feature=youtu.be)

217.

Slime mold grew a network similar to the Tokyo Rail system.

Reference: (https://www.wired.com/2010/01/slime-mold-grows-network-just-like-tokyo-rail-system/)

218.

There is a name for that amazing and relaxing tingling feeling you get at random times, autonomous sensory meridian response.

Reference:
(https://en.wikipedia.org/wiki/Autonomous_sensory_meridian_response)

219.

There is an actual place called Snowflake, Arizona, where people with sensitivities can go to live in peace.

Reference:
(https://www.youtube.com/watch?v=sMzEmvv48pE&feature=youtu
.be)

220.

While the Amish don't allow themselves to drive, there is a slowly growing market for them to bend the rules with in the form of "Amish Taxi Drivers".

Reference: (http://amishamerica.com/an-inside-look-at-amish-taxi-driving/)

221.

There is a group of Japanese macaques that engage in sexual behaviors with Sifka deer.

Reference: (https://www.npr.org/sections/thetwo-way/2017/12/15/571175252/scientists-say-japanese-monkeys-are-having-sexual-interactions-with-deer)

222.

Midnight Cowboy is the only X rated movie to win an Oscar.

Reference: (http://www.mtv.com/news/2767359/whats-the-big-deal-midnight-cowboy-1969/)

223.

Martin Luther King Jr. was a "Trekkie" and implored Nichelle Nichols not to leave the show.

Reference: (https://www.npr.org/2011/01/17/132942461/Star-Treks-Uhura-Reflects-On-MLK-Encounter)

224.

Cork is a layer of bark tissue that is harvested for commercial use, primarily from Quercus suber. About half of the world's supply of cork is produced in Portugal. Cork was examined microscopically by Robert Hooke, which led to his discovery and naming of the cell.

Reference: (https://en.wikipedia.org/wiki/Cork_(material))

225.

The FBI estimates that there are between twenty five and fifty serial killers operating throughout the United States at any given time.

Reference: (https://www.scientificamerican.com/article/5-myths-about-serial-killers-and-why-they-persist-excerpt/)

226.

During an annual Peruvian street-fighting event named "Takanakuy", members of the community must call out their opponent by first and last name before fighting them in a circle to settle personal conflicts.

Reference: (https://en.wikipedia.org/wiki/Takanakuy)

227.

If you are someone whose shoelaces are constantly coming undone you are probably using a "weak" version of the traditional "bunny ears" knot. Once you switch to the strong version, the likelihood of the knot coming undone with activity and time diminishes significantly.

Reference:
(https://www.ted.com/talks/terry_moore_how_to_tie_your_shoes)

228.

On July 6th, 1962, Lawrence Livermore National Lab detonated the Sedan thermonuclear device under the surface of Yucca Flat, Nevada, to test whether nuclear explosives could be effectively used in earthmoving; the concept was abandoned due to intense fallout.

Reference: (https://www.youtube.com/watch?v=ssLZ4bUTDYM)

229.

The first shipping container was invented and patented in 1956 by the owner of an American trucking fleet, which reduced his shipping cost from $5.86 to .16 cents, paving the way for globalization and mass intercontinental shipping.

Reference: (http://www.priceandspeed.com.au/about-us/history-shipping-containers/)

230.

Based on a University of Toronto study, our mood can actually change how our visual cortex processes information.

Reference: (http://www.artsci.utoronto.ca/main/news-archives/people-who-wear-rose-coloured-glasses-see-more/)

231.

The near-extinction of the American bison was a deliberate plan by the U.S. Army to starve Native Americans into submission. One colonel told a hunter who felt guilty shooting 30 bulls in one trip, "Kill every buffalo you can! Every buffalo dead is an Indian gone."

Reference:
(https://www.theatlantic.com/national/archive/2016/05/the-buffalo-killers/482349/)

232.

Friday the 13th is considered to be an unlucky day, but the truth is that it is safer to travel that day. So, if you want to be surer that no accident will occur, travel then.

Reference: (https://www.reuters.com/article/us-luck-odd/friday-13th-not-more-unlucky-study-shows-idUSHER25778420080612)

233.

The European Wall Lizard can detach its tail and later regrow it. This is a defense mechanism referred to as autotomy.

Reference: (https://bygl.osu.edu/index.php/node/585)

234.

There is an ancient Persian method of execution called Scaphism. The word comes from Greek, meaning, "anything scooped (or hollowed) out". It entailed trapping the victim inside two boats, feeding and covering him with milk and honey, and allowing him to fester and be devoured by vermin.

Reference: (https://en.wikipedia.org/wiki/Scaphism)

235.

Mice have a giant neuron that wraps around their entire brain.

Reference: (https://www.nature.com/news/a-giant-neuron-found-wrapped-around-entire-mouse-brain-1.21539)

236.

Proceeds from the Pink Floyd album The Dark Side of the Moon went towards funding the film "Monty Python and the Holy Grail." Also, the members of the band were a fan of the comedy troupe, and often took breaks in the middle of their recording sessions to watch Monty Python's Flying Circus.

Reference: (https://www.rollingstone.com/music/music-features/pink-floyds-dark-side-of-the-moon-10-things-you-didnt-know-201743/)

237.

Game designer Will Wright was inspired to create The Sims by the 1991 Oakland firestorm. He lost his home in the fire, and wanted to create a game that emulated his experience of rebuilding his life in the aftermath.

Reference:
(https://en.wikipedia.org/wiki/Will_Wright_(game_designer))

238.

There was an earthquake so great in New Madrid that it caused the Mississippi river to flow backwards temporarily.

Reference:(https://en.wikipedia.org/wiki/1811%E2%80%9312_New_Madrid_earthquakes#Eyewitness_accounts)

239.

The brain doesn't firmly distinguish between physical pain and intense emotional pain. So the same brain networks that are activated when you're burned by hot coffee also light up when you think about an ex who dumped you.

Reference:(http://www.cnn.com/2011/HEALTH/03/28/burn.heartbreak.same.to.brain/index.html)

240.

Only 3 bowlers have picked up the 7-10 split on television and despite many shows and movies showing it being picked up by directly sliding one pin into another, this is, in fact, impossible.

Reference:
(https://en.wikipedia.org/wiki/Split_(bowling)#7%E2%80%9310_split)

241.

Two thirds of Arsenic in the air is from human causes.

Reference: (https://www.greenfacts.org/en/arsenic/index.htm)

242.

If two brothers marry two sisters, their offspring will not only be first cousins, but they will be double first cousins, as in they share both sets of grandparents.

Reference: (https://www.bhg.com/health-family/reunions/activities/cousins-chart/)

243.

A "Ladies Carousel" was a popular sport in Vienna. The ladies, on horsebacks or in carriages, had to lunge with a sword at models of Turks' heads made of papier mâché impaled on poles.

Reference: (http://www.habsburger.net/en/chapter/impaling-turks-heads-court?language=en)

244.

In Thailand, the lèse-majesté laws are so strict that in 2015 a Thai factory worker faced 37 years in jail for mocking the Thai king's dog on Facebook.

Reference: (https://www.theguardian.com/world/2015/dec/15/thai-man-faces-jail-insulting-kings-dog-sarcastic-internet-post)

245.

Some hospitals now have a "No Nicotine" policy for new hires, which includes not only cigarettes but dip, vape, nicotine patches and gum.

Reference: (http://katv.com/archive/arkansas-hospital-taking-stand-against-hiring-tobacco-users)

246.

Archibald McCafferty, an Australian serial killer who murdered four people, including a fellow prisoner, was paroled in 1997, after serving 23 years, and deported to Scotland. In 1998, he threatened to kill two police officers who pulled him over for drunk driving, and received probation.

Reference: (http://murderpedia.org/male.M/m/mccafferty-archibald.htm)

247.

Aum Shinryko, the Japanese death cult, did not perform the first private nuclear weapon test in the Outback in 1993.

Reference: (https://www.vice.com/en_ca/article/7xkv7q/did-a-japanese-cult-detonate-a-nuclear-bomb-in-the-australian-desert)

248.

The sperm of ants and bees do battle inside the queens.

Reference: (https://www.nationalgeographic.com/science/phenomena/2010/03/18/sperm-war-the-sperm-of-ants-and-bees-do-battle-inside-the-queens/)

249.

Smash Mouth's first hit single, "Walkin' on the Sun", is a political song, calling for racial justice in the wake of the Rodney King beating.

Reference: (https://en.wikipedia.org/wiki/Walkin%27_on_the_Sun#Lyrical_theme)

250.

Pill bugs are actually crustaceans that adapted to live entirely on land.

Reference: (https://www.pestworld.org/pest-guide/occasional-invaders/pillbugs/)

251.

In Guatemala, an estimated 40% to 60% of the population still speak a Mayan language.

Reference:
(https://en.wikipedia.org/wiki/Mayan_languages#Distribution)

252.

In Detroit, in 2012, a gunfight broke out during an argument over who makes the best Kool-Aid.

Reference: (https://www.huffingtonpost.ca/entry/kool-aid-gun-fight-shooting-detroit_n_1559612)

253.

The original Stormtrooper and Rebel Alliance armors were made of vacuum-formed plastics by Andrew Ainsworth.

Reference: (http://www.starwarshelmets.com/Original-stormtrooper-armor-helmets.htm)

254.

The Freedom of Panorama is a provisional law that permits taking photographs and video footage and creating other images of buildings and sometimes sculptures and other art works which are permanently located in a public place.

Reference: (https://en.wikipedia.org/wiki/Freedom_of_panorama)

255.

During the "Petticoat duel", in 1792, Lady Almeria Braddock challenged Mrs. Elphinstone to a duel in London's Hyde Park over remarks the latter made about the former's true age; they dueled with pistols, then with swords, until Mrs. Elphinstone agreed to write Lady Almeria an apology.

Reference: (https://en.wikipedia.org/wiki/List_of_duels)

256.

American Psycho author Bret Easton Ellis tried to order cocaine from his dealer but instead of texting him he tweeted it to his followers by accident.

Reference: (http://the-talks.com/interview/bret-easton-ellis/)

257.

After the conclusion of the First World War, the French government declared a "Zone Rouge" deemed unfit for human habitation.

Reference: (https://en.wikipedia.org/wiki/Zone_Rouge)

258.

The Creation Museum explains historical events and artifacts through Biblical interpretation. One of their findings is that the dinosaurs were wiped out by Noah's flood.

Reference: (https://creationmuseum.org/dinosaurs-dragons/allosaurus/)

259.

Indian holy man, Sadu Mahant Amar Shantaram, has kept his right hand raised for the last 42 years.

Reference:(http://www.knowledgeroof.com/details.php?id=235&category=storyfeed&title=OMG!!-For-42-Years,-This-Sadhu-Has-Kept-His-Right-Hand-Raised)

260.

A gravity hill, also known as a magnetic hill, or anti-gravity hill, is a place where the layout of the surrounding land produces an optical illusion, making a slight downhill slope appear to be an uphill slope.

Thus, a car left out of gear will appear to be rolling uphill against gravity.

Reference: (https://en.wikipedia.org/wiki/Gravity_hill)

261.

The oldest American TV show currently in production is "Meet the Press." The oldest sports TV show currently in production is "PGA Tour" on CBS.

Reference:(https://en.wikipedia.org/wiki/List_of_American_television_programs_currently_in_production)

262.

German engineer Bernd Brandes volunteered to be killed and eaten by aspiring cannibal Armin Meiwes, who placed an ad on the internet looking for someone to be killed and eaten. After eating Brandes and going to jail, Meiwes became a vegetarian.

Reference: (https://en.wikipedia.org/wiki/Armin_Meiwes)

263.

Bills of Mortality were statistics distributed in London starting in the late-16th century during the time of the plague to monitor burials. These statistics were gathered by the Worshipful Company of Parish Clerks and later included information such as cause of death and the person's age.

Reference: (https://en.wikipedia.org/wiki/Bills_of_mortality)

264.

Bob Marley's offspring have 8 Grammy awards to their name.

Reference:
(https://en.wikipedia.org/wiki/Stephen_Marley_(musician))

265.

The adult male tapir from Costa Rica has seriously large genitalia. Their erection gets kicked about as it walks.

Reference: (https://youtu.be/xf5oMcQaby0)

266.

The term "computer bug" came from the earliest computer engineers finding literal bugs inside their computer relay switches that prevented the switches from closing properly and completing an operation.

Reference: (https://www.youtube.com/watch?v=LN0ucKNX0hc)

267.

In 2013, an app was created to help Icelanders avoid accidental incest.

Reference: (https://www.usatoday.com/story/tech/2013/04/18/new-app-helps-icelanders-avoid-accidental-incest/2093649/)

268.

The Tory party in the U.K. got its name from the Middle Irish word "tóraidhe", which means outlaw, robber or brigand.

Reference: (https://en.wikipedia.org/wiki/Tory#History)

269.

Chocolate contains a large number of Theobromine, a substance that could cause women's period pain more noticeable.

Reference: (http://blog.hersday.com/2018/04/14/what-causes-period-pain-chocolate-seriously/)

270.

You actually weigh more at the South and North Poles than if you'd stand on the equator in Ecuador.

Reference: (http://curious.astro.cornell.edu/about-us/42-our-solar-system/the-earth/gravity/94-does-your-weight-change-between-the-poles-and-the-equator-intermediate)

271.

The longest sperm cells of any organism are produced by the fruit fly Drosophila bifurca, with tails reaching nearly 6 centimeters in length, several times longer than the fly itself.

Reference: (https://www.sciencedirect.com/science/article/pii/S0960982206016149)

272.

Greyfriars Bobby was a Skye terrier who became known in 19th-century Edinburgh for spending 14 years guarding the grave of his owner until he died himself on January 14th, 1872.

Reference: (https://en.wikipedia.org/wiki/Greyfriars_Bobby)

273.

The Finnish Air Force Academy still uses a swastika on its flag, as this kind of cross was used by the Sami shamans in pre-Christian Finland in relation with Horagalles, the Thunder God.

Reference: (https://en.wikipedia.org/wiki/Air_Force_Academy,_Finnish_Air_Force)

274.

Warren Harding led the first group that climbed El Capitan in Yosemite. The climb took 45 days and more than 3,400 feet of climbing. This was partially because he, while climbing, would often

drink excessively and be too drunk to climb, needing to be lowered
to ground again.

Reference:
(https://en.wikipedia.org/wiki/Warren_Harding_(climber)#The_Nos
e)

275.

In Washington State, miniature horses must be allowed as service
animals in food establishments.

Reference: (https://app.leg.wa.gov/rcw/default.aspx?cite=49.60.218)

276.

Most cheeses are not vegetarian because they contain an ingredient,
rennet, which is usually made from animal stomachs.

Reference: (https://www.formaggiokitchen.com/blog/the-rennet-
story-animal-vegetable-and-microbial/)

277.

Dogs can detect humans buried 12 feet underground.

Reference: (http://www.philly.com/philly/news/bucks-missing-men-
cadaver-dogs-12-feet-underground-20170713.html)

278.

Gibbons have also been observed using tools, with clear differences
in the male and female's capacity to learn.

Reference: (https://onekindplanet.org/animal-behaviour/tool-
use/tool-use-in-gibbons/)

279.

David Boreanaz was in Dido's "White Flag" video.

Reference: (https://www.youtube.com/watch?v=j-fWDrZSiZs)

280.

The Arizona Beverage company roots trace back to 1971, when friends John Ferolito and Don Vultaggio opened a beverage distribution business in Brooklyn, New York. The company was a successful beer distributor. In 1992, they produced the first bottles of their own Arizona teas.

Reference:
(https://en.wikipedia.org/wiki/Arizona_Beverage_Company)

281.

Human zoos were a thing back in the day in Europe where they would have natives from Africa and Asia as the "public exhibitions of humans."

Reference: (https://en.wikipedia.org/wiki/Human_zoo)

282.

The Alaskan town of Glacier View doesn't get dark enough for fireworks on the 4th of July. Instead, they drive cars off a cliff.

Reference:
(https://www.youtube.com/watch?v=KbMYzMUu06Q&feature=youtu.be)

283.

About 15 percent of the world's population has a significant physical or mental disability, including about 5 percent of children.

Reference: (https://www.cbsnews.com/news/15-worldwide-have-physical-or-mental-disability/)

284.

An Arizona TV station owner was concerned about the negative connotations "D.W.I." had in his station's call letters KDWI, so he changed his station's name to KGUN.

Reference: (https://en.wikipedia.org/wiki/KGUN-TV)

285.

If you've ever wanted to watch hundreds of men and women run down a hill while chasing a wheel of cheese, then Cooper Hill Cheese Roll is the place to be. The exact origin of the cheese rolling isn't known, but is believed to have started in the early 1800s.

Reference: (https://radseason.com/event/coopers-hill-cheese-rolling-gloucester-united-kingdom/)

286.

Despite being 99% of the actual mass of an atom, the nucleus is very small. So small that it can be compared to a pea in the middle of a racetrack, or a fly in the middle of a cathedral.

Reference: (http://academic.brooklyn.cuny.edu/physics/sobel/Nucphys/atomprop.html)

287.

Pat Morita was made an honorary member of the 442nd Regiment, Mr. Miyagi's World War II unit.

Reference: (http://encyclopedia.densho.org/Pat_Morita/)

288.

CIPA is an extremely rare condition where a person feels no pain, heat, cold, or any nerve-related sensations.

Reference: (https://brainworldmagazine.com/feeling-no-pain-like-live-cipa)

289.

In places where it's been measured, the biomass of flying insects has declined by more than 75% over the last 27 years.

Reference:
(http://journals.plos.org/plosone/article?id=10.1371/journal.pone.0185809)

290.

China's biggest agricultural export are onions.

Reference: (https://atlas.media.mit.edu/en/profile/country/chn/)

291.

A Portland, Oregon, woman strangled a hitman with her bare hands.

Reference: (http://abc7.com/news/portland-woman-strangles-hitman-w--bare-hands/31994/)

292.

Package delivery slips in Japan have braille and other physical markers for visually impaired customers.

Reference: (https://www.accessible-japan.com/braille-on-japanese-delivery-notice/)

293.

The Vatican once dispatched a church father to personally verify if Shirley Temple was a 30-year-old dwarf with false teeth in a wig.

Reference:
(https://en.wikipedia.org/wiki/Shirley_Temple#Myths_and_rumors)

294.

In the mid-1970s, a lawyer from Akron, Ohio, wrote the Cleveland Browns football team with a complaint about paper airplanes being tossed around the stadium. The Browns replied with a letter saying, "I feel that you should be aware that some asshole is signing your name to stupid letters."

Reference:
(http://www.abajournal.com/gallery/cease_and_desist_letters_gallery/1752)

295.

There is a disease called Testicular Torsion, which is when your testicle cord twists.

Reference: (https://www.healthline.com/health/testicular-torsion)

296.

The Hudson River Chain, or "Great Chain," is a chain that the Continental Army strung up to prevent the British Navy from sailing upriver during the American Revolution.

Reference: (http://www.fortwiki.com/Great_Chain_-_West_Point)

297.

The construction crew working at the Medical College of Georgia in Augusta found thousands of human bones in the Old Medical College Building basement.

Reference: (https://www.atlasobscura.com/articles/bodies-in-the-basement-the-forgotten-bones-of-america-s-medical-schools)

298.

The earliest form of football, as acknowledged by FIFA, was played in ancient Han dynasty China and was called Cuju.

Reference: (https://en.wikipedia.org/wiki/Cuju)

299.

Huddles before a play in American Football were started by a deaf football team.

Reference: (http://www.lifeprint.com/asl101/topics/football-02.htm)

300.

When Robert Downey Jr. was sent to prison he wanted to tell his son that he was going off to Yugoslavia to learn how to be a spy.

Reference: (https://www.vanityfair.com/hollywood/2000/08/robert-downey-jr-prison)

301.

Navajo Hogans, or mud huts, have a gender. Female Hogans are round shaped like "a pregnant women" and are used to live in. Male Hogans are slanted and pointy and are used for more "manly things" like tribe meetings and rituals.

Reference: (https://hikearizona.com/dexcoder.php?PID=344)

302.

The most visited place in Europe is Disneyland Paris with 14 million people each year.

Reference: (http://en.rfi.fr/france/20120406-disneyland-paris-europes-top-tourist-destination)

303.

During the Cold War, the United States began operation Davy (C)rockett: a program tasked with creating a mobile nuclear rocket launcher that could be fired with 1 or 2 man teams.

Reference:
(https://www.militaryfactory.com/smallarms/detail.asp?smallarms_id=570)

304.

In 2017, America overtook Mexico again as the most obese nation in the world with estimates that 50% of the nation will be obese by 2030.

Reference: (https://www.marketwatch.com/story/the-us-is-the-most-obese-nation-in-the-world-just-ahead-of-mexico-2017-05-19)

305.

Morarji Desai, the 4th Prime Minister of India, was an avid practitioner of urine therapy and attributed his longevity to drinking urine, which he called the "water of life", at least twice every day.

Reference: (https://www.independent.co.uk/news/people/obituary-morarji-desai-1615165.html)

306.

Jack Black first acted in a television commercial at age 13 for the video game Pitfall.

Reference: (https://en.wikipedia.org/wiki/Jack_Black)

307.

In 1995, David Justice had a higher batting average than Derek Jeter. In 1996, Justice also had a higher average than Jeter, and in 1997, Justice again had a higher average than Jeter. However, overall three years combined, Derek Jeter had the higher batting average.

Reference:
(http://flawofaverages.com/book/Chapter18/Chapter18.html)

308.

The Zildjian music company was founded by an alchemist trying to turn base metals into gold.

Reference:
(https://en.wikipedia.org/wiki/Avedis_Zildjian_Company)

309.

One of the founders of the Aldi supermarket chain was kidnapped for 17 days until a 7 million Deutsche Mark was paid by a bishop.

Reference:
(https://www.telegraph.co.uk/news/worldnews/europe/germany/7915877/Aldis-reclusive-founder-dies-age-88.html)

310.

In the city of Lakewood, California, a post-World War II suburban community, developers in the city built 17,500 homes in less than three years on empty fields. They then sold about 30 homes per day to war veterans backed by government mortgages, once selling 107 homes in one hour.

Reference: (https://en.wikipedia.org/wiki/Lakewood,_California)

311.

There are only 13 active advertising blimps in the world.

Reference: (http://www.vanwagneraerial.com/blog/18-blimp-facts-for-the-average-av-geek)

312.

Kaliningrad Oblast is a detached part of Russia which borders Poland.

Reference: (https://en.wikipedia.org/wiki/Kaliningrad_Oblast)

313.

In 1982, Vangelis, the famous composer, composed the evening news opening theme for the Greek national TV channel. The track is still in use today.

Reference: (https://www.youtube.com/watch?v=ah7sSGiLkck)

314.

In the 1950s and 1960s, Canada spent "thousands and thousands" making a "gaydar" to detect homosexual government employees.

Reference: (https://nationalpost.com/news/canada/the-fruit-machine/amp)

315.

The fax machine was invented the same year as the great migration on the Oregon Trail began.

Reference: (http://www.mandatory.com/living/1285087-fax-machine-history)

316.

Years divisible by 100 are not leap years, unless they are also divisible by 400.

Reference: (https://en.wikipedia.org/wiki/Leap_year)

317.

A transmissible form of cancer affects dogs. The tumor cells themselves are the infectious agent, and are not related to the dog hosts. The cells seem to originate from a dog that lived 11,000 years ago, making it the oldest continually propagated cell line in the world.

Reference:
(https://en.wikipedia.org/wiki/Canine_transmissible_venereal_tumor#Biology)

318.

There is a medical condition called auto-brewery syndrome where the afflicted becomes drunk after the consumption of too many carbohydrates. It has been used as a drunk driving defense.

Reference: (https://wikipedia.org/wiki/Auto-brewery_syndrome)

319.

Babur, founder of the Mughal dynasty in India which ruled from 1526 to 1857, was born in Uzbekistan, to a father related to Tamerlane and a mother related to Genghis Khan.

Reference: (https://en.wikipedia.org/wiki/Babur)

320.

The first democratically elected communist government, other than San Marino's, came into power in 1957. It was the CPI, the Communist Party of India, which set up a still-functioning communist government in Kerala.

Reference: (https://en.wikipedia.org/wiki/E._M._S._Namboodiripad)

321.

The lead singer of the Ska band The Aquabats is the creator of the kids television show "Yo Gabba Gabba!"

Reference: (https://en.wikipedia.org/wiki/Yo_Gabba_Gabba!)

322.

Hedgehogs can suffer from a rare disease called "balloon syndrome," which causes them to inflate like a beach ball.

Reference: (https://en.wikipedia.org/wiki/Hedgehog#Diseases)

323.

In the theatrical release of "Bruce Almighty," God pages Bruce using a real phone number. The owners of the number, which included a church in North Carolina, got hundreds of phone calls from people wanting to talk to God. The TV and video versions were edited to show the fictional 555 exchange.

Reference:
(https://en.wikipedia.org/wiki/Bruce_Almighty#Controversy)

324.

Rob Thomas originally had George Michael in mind as the vocalist for Santana's hit song "Smooth". However, when Thomas recorded a demo, Santana enjoyed it and decided to have him record the final version.

Reference: (https://en.wikipedia.org/wiki/Smooth_(Santana_song))

325.

Female hysteria used to be treated by masturbating the patients to orgasm. This is called hysterical paroxysm.

Reference:
(https://en.wikipedia.org/wiki/Female_hysteria#19th_century)

326.

Ed Pulaski saved his all but 5 of his 45 man crew in the Great Fire of 1910 by ordering them into a mineshaft as the wildfire overran their position.

Reference: (https://en.wikipedia.org/wiki/Ed_Pulaski)

327.

In 1938, Ronald Reagan tried to join the Communist Party in California, but was rejected due to personal traits, including patriotism.

Reference: (http://www.newyorker.com/magazine/2004/06/28/the-unknowable)

328.

The Colorado River's delta is mostly dry, thanks to heavy use of water upstream. It's now mostly been consumed by the Sonora Desert.

Reference: (https://en.wikipedia.org/wiki/Colorado_River_Delta)

329.

The record for the greatest 24-hour temperature change ever recorded on earth occurred in 1972 in Loma, Montana when the temperature rose from -54°F (-47°C) on January 14th to 49°F (9°C) on January 15th: an astonishing 103°F (56°C) rise.

Reference:(https://maps.wunderground.com/blog/weatherhistorian/comment.html?entrynum=101)

330.

The Ultimate Coast to Coast challenge is a 5,500 mile ride that starts at Key West, Florida, and goes up to the Arctic Circle to the town Deadhorse, Alaska.

Reference: (http://www.ironbutt.com/rides/ultimate.htm)

331.

Yoko Ono's uncle, Toshikazu Kase, was a high ranking Japanese official during World War II and he was featured in the BBC Documentary "The World At War."

Reference: (https://en.wikipedia.org/wiki/Toshikazu_Kase)

332.

Some otters juggle rocks.

Reference: (http://geekologie.com/2017/12/happy-otter-juggles-rocks-in-excitement.php)

333.

"Petty treason" is committed against your lawful superior, as opposed to "High treason," which is against the state or sovereign.

Reference: (https://en.wikipedia.org/wiki/Petty_treason)

334.

1 day old baby reindeer are faster than an Olympic sprinter.

Reference:
(https://en.wikipedia.org/wiki/Reindeer#Social_structure,_migration_and_range)

335.

There is an actual "Sleeping Beauty" syndrome, which is a rare sleep disorder characterized by persistent episodic hypersomnia and cognitive or mood changes. Individuals with the disorder experience recurring episodes of prolonged sleep, 15 to 21 hours a day, and cannot remember weeks at a time.

Reference:
(https://en.wikipedia.org/wiki/Kleine%E2%80%93Levin_syndrome)

336.

Early on in the Popeye the Sailor Man's comic, Popeye didn't eat spinach to gain strength. Instead, he rubbed the head of a magic chicken.

Reference: (https://en.wikipedia.org/wiki/Popeye)

337.

The word "orange" was derived from the type of tree that grow oranges; before, the color was known only as "red-yellow".

Reference: (https://youtu.be/xn7ZaT3AgoU)

338.

Kobe Bryant once bet $500,000 on a free-throw.

Reference: (https://www.youtube.com/watch?v=Oii6_-56YI0)

339.

During the construction of the Metro Red Line subway in Los Angeles, 2,000 fossils were discovered, some as old as 16.5 million years old. These included 39 species of extinct marine fish that had never before been discovered.

Reference:
(https://en.wikipedia.org/wiki/Red_Line_(Los_Angeles_Metro))

340.

Pegasus, the mythical divine stallion, is the son of Poseidon and is said to have been born from the blood of Medusa.

Reference: (https://en.wikipedia.org/wiki/Pegasus#Birth)

341.

A Quasi-star is a type of extremely massive star that may have existed early in the universe. Its energy would come from material falling into a central black hole, as opposed to nuclear fusion.

Reference: (https://en.wikipedia.org/wiki/Quasi-star)

342.

Half of strictly protected forests in Europe are located in Finland.

Reference: (http://www.metla.fi/metinfo/sustainability/finnish-protected-forests.htm)

343.

The East India Company used the Revolutionary War to take French possessions in India.

Reference:
(https://en.wikipedia.org/wiki/American_Revolutionary_War#India)

344.

Four people have died searching for a treasure hidden by a millionaire in 2009 in the southwestern Rocky Mountains. The estimated $2 million treasure has yet to be discovered and its whereabouts are contained within a cryptic poem that the millionaire wrote after he hid his treasure.

Reference: (https://www.youtube.com/watch?v=_MV7CQPC53M)

345.

Musicians Nikki Sixx, Sir-Mix-a-Lot, Ryan Lewis, Duff McKagan, and Mike McCready all went to the same Seattle high school. Actress Rose McGowan also went there.

Reference:
(https://en.wikipedia.org/wiki/Roosevelt_High_School_(Seattle))

346.

The term "Jiffy" was defined by Gilbert Newton Lewis. He proposed a unit of time called the "jiffy", which was equal to the time it takes light to travel one centimeter in a vacuum, or approximately 33.3564 picoseconds.

Reference: (https://en.wikipedia.org/wiki/Jiffy_(time))

347.

The Hubble Limit represents the furthest observable objects in the universe as anything beyond it is accelerating away faster than the light it emits. Since the universe is expanding we could forever lose sight of the furthest objects.

Reference: (https://wikipedia.org/wiki/Hubble_volume)

348.

Whales can explode from the gases created from decomposition, sending guts and blood around 160 feet, or 50 meters, at about 43 miles per hour, or 70 kilometers per hour.

Reference: (https://youtu.be/X_6Q38CFYBw)

349.

The earliest picture of a yo-yo is on an ancient Greek vase from 440BC.

Reference: (http://greece.greekreporter.com/2018/04/08/the-ancient-greek-boy-and-his-yo-yo/)

350.

In 1950, the crew of a bulk freight carrier propelled it with an improvised sail when the engine went out; it was the last use of the sail for bulk freight ships.

Reference: (https://en.wikipedia.org/wiki/SS_Tobruk)

351.

A woman put cyanide in pill bottles of Excedrin and placed them on the shelves of stores. This led to the deaths of her husband and a 40 year old woman.

Reference: (http://www.history.com/this-day-in-history/woman-convicted-for-tampering-with-excedrin)

352.

The screenwriters for the film "Alien" pitched the movie to various studios as, "Jaws' in space".

Reference: (https://en.wikipedia.org/wiki/Alien_(film))

353.

Platinum was first discovered and worked by Pre-Columbian Amerindian tribes in the Chóco rainforest, using a sophisticated method of powder metallurgy.

Reference: (https://en.wikipedia.org/wiki/Platinum)

354.

Raw chicken is now linked to paralysis in dogs, including chicken neck treats.

Reference: (https://pursuit.unimelb.edu.au/articles/raw-chicken-linked-to-paralysis-in-dogs?utm_source=twiter&utm_medium=social&utm_content=story)

355.

There is a sequel novel to "Forrest Gump," in which he captures Saddam Hussein and Jenny dies and becomes a ghost.

Reference: (https://en.wikipedia.org/wiki/Gump_and_Co.)

356.

The Banana slug "Ariolimax dolichophallus", has a penis that can be 6 to 8 inches long. After sex, the male slug eats its own penis.

Reference: (https://www.wired.com/2015/09/absurd-creature-week-slug-big-penis-mate-upside/)

357.

The English words "cannabis" and "canvas" come from the same Scythian, or Thracian, word.

Reference: (https://en.wikipedia.org/wiki/Etymology_of_cannabis)

358.

In the Middle Ages, it was an accepted political act for two kings to sleep in the same bed as a symbol of unity between their two countries; much like the modern day photo-op.

Reference:
(https://www.telegraph.co.uk/news/uknews/1582009/Richard-I-slept-with-French-king-but-not-gay.html)

359.

In 1672, a Dutch mob murdered and ate their Prime Minister, John de Witt. One was said to have feasted on his eyeball.

Reference: (https://www.historyextra.com/period/is-it-true-that-an-angry-mob-of-dutchmen-killed-and-ate-their-own-prime-minister-in-1672/)

360.

It's possible to create a black hole formed from radiation as opposed to matter.

Reference: (https://en.wikipedia.org/wiki/Kugelblitz_(astrophysics))

361.

During World War I, London was protected by massive lengths of steel cables suspended from observation balloons to guard against air raids. These "balloon aprons" forced pilots to fly above their range or too low to avoid AA fire.

Reference: (https://mashable.com/2016/03/02/wwi-balloons/#02B7Fnpq48qs)

362.

For the airplane landing scene in "Bonfire of the Vanities," Second Unit Director Eric Schwab calculated the moment when a runway at John F. Kennedy Airport would line up exactly with the setting sun and managed to film in the single 30-second time period when this occurs in a year.

Reference:
(https://en.wikipedia.org/wiki/The_Bonfire_of_the_Vanities_(film))

363.

Auntie Anne's local pretzel flavors around the world include seaweed, banana, and date.

Reference: (https://thefreshtoast.com/culture/how-the-pretzel-went-from-soft-to-hard/)

364.

Queen Elizabeth II, by the Grace of God Queen of Australia and Her other Realms and Territories, Head of the Commonwealth is also the Duke of Lancaster.

Reference: (https://en.wikipedia.org/wiki/Duchy_of_Lancaster)

365.

One company owns or holds a majority stake in Keurig Green Mountain, Krispy Kreme Doughnuts, Panera Bread, The Dr. Pepper Snapple Group, Peet's Coffee & Tea, Caribou Coffee Company, Eistein Bagels, Espresso House, Mighty Leaf Tea, Stumptown Coffee, and Bruegger's Bagels.

Reference: (https://en.wikipedia.org/wiki/JAB_Holding_Company)

366.

Kermit the Frog has a doctorate in Amphibian Letters, for his efforts in environmentalism.

Reference:
(https://www.telegraph.co.uk/education/universityeducation/8855284/Surprising-honorary-degree-recipients.html?image=3)

367.

A group of barmen is called a "promise of barmen."

Reference: (https://didyouknow.org/lists/collective-nouns-of-people/)

368.

Tejano music, or Tex-Mex music, is the name given to various forms of folk and popular music originating among the Mexican-American populations of Central and Southern Texas.

Reference: (https://en.wikipedia.org/wiki/Tejano_music)

369.

Oman holds jurisdiction over an enclave of land within the United Arab Emirates who in turn holds jurisdiction over a smaller piece of territory within that enclave.

Reference: (https://bigthink.com/strange-maps/60-madha-and-nahwa)

370.

Quidditch World Cup is a real thing and that U.S. has won the cup 3 out of 4 times that it has been held.

Reference: (https://en.wikipedia.org/wiki/IQA_World_Cup)

371.

There are negative Kelvin temperatures. They are actually hotter than positive ones.

Reference: (https://www.mpg.de/research/negative-absolute-temperature)

372.

The phrase "bless you" originated as a prayer for people dying from the bubonic plague in the sixth century.

Reference: (https://people.howstuffworks.com/sneezing.htm)

373.

A study about class differences in 18th and 19th century England showed that on average, a wealthy 16-year old boy was 8.5 inches taller than a poor 16-year old boy, as a result of malnourishment and living standards.

Reference:
(https://www.emeraldinsight.com/doi/abs/10.1016/S0363-3268%2807%2925003-7)

374.

74.55% of Miami's population speaks a language other than English at home.

Reference: (https://en.wikipedia.org/wiki/Miami#Languages)

375.

Some aircraft carriers can produce hundreds of thousands of freshwater through a process called desalination. This can be used to help provide relief to cities recovering from disasters.

Reference:
(https://adventure.howstuffworks.com/survival/wilderness/convert-salt-water1.htm)

376.

H.G. Wells, author of The Time Machine, wrote a rulebook for a tabletop wargame called "Little Wars."

Reference: (https://en.wikipedia.org/wiki/Little_Wars)

377.

During World War II, the Germans captured one of Joseph Stalin's sons. They offered to exchange him for the captured German Field Marshall Friedrich Paulus. Stalin refused, saying "I will not trade a Field Marshall for a Lieutenant."

Reference:
(https://www.independent.co.uk/news/world/europe/joseph-stalin-s-hated-son-surrendered-to-the-nazis-archives-reveal-8498745.html)

378.

George Washington illegally rotated his enslaved personal chef, Hercules, between the Capitol and Mount Vernon to avoid laws that would free him. Hercules eventually escaped to freedom.

Reference: (https://en.wikipedia.org/wiki/Hercules_(chef))

379.

Poachers are now hacking into tags that conservationists put on endangered animals to track them.

Reference: (https://www.smithsonianmag.com/smart-news/tracking-collars-poachers-animals-scientists-180962345/)

380.

Holi or "Festival of Love" is considered as one of the most revered and celebrated festivals of India and it is celebrated in almost every part of the country. It is the day people get to unite together forgetting all resentments and all types of bad feelings towards each other.

Reference: (https://www.holifestival.org/)

381.

Horses sleep standing up by using a stay apparatus, which is an adaptation of the musculoskeletal system that enables them to lock their limbs in place. They do lie down occasionally though as sleeping standing up only allows for light sleep.

Reference: (https://onekindplanet.org/top-10/unusual-sleeping-habits/)

382.

David Bowie wrote the song "TVC-15" about Iggy Pop's drug-fueled hallucination that his girlfriend was being swallowed whole by Bowie's television.

Reference: (https://en.wikipedia.org/wiki/TVC_15)

383.

In the city of Geneva, there is an annual tradition of smashing chocolate cauldrons on the ground to commemorate the time when a Genevan woman killed an enemy soldier in a siege by dropping a pot of boiling soup onto his head.

Reference: (https://en.wikipedia.org/wiki/L%27Escalade)

384.

The Giver was inspired by Lois Lowry sneaking out of Washington Heights, a U.S. Air Force housing complex in Tokyo, to explore Shibuya and the surrounding areas.

Reference:
(https://en.wikipedia.org/wiki/Washington_Heights_(Tokyo))

385.

Remnants of the legs of the wicker man burned in the 1973 movie are still visible in Burrowhead, Galloway to this day. Now only stumps, the legs were stolen by a thief in a truck whose identity remains a mystery.

Reference:
(http://www.nothingtoseehere.net/2006/08/the_wicker_mans_legs_burrowhea.html)

386.

Llanfairpwll is not the original name of the town in Wales, and may have been an early example of people adding to the name to attract tourists.

Reference: (http://www.businessinsider.com/welsh-town-has-the-longest-name-in-europe-2015-9)

387.

Tunnel Rats were the men who infiltrated Vietcong tunnels during the Vietnam War. Once underground, they faced many deadly traps while crawling through the darkness: pungee spike pit falls, mines and boxes of scorpions attached to trip wires, snakes tethered to the tunnel walls, and much more.

Reference: (https://warhistoryonline.com/vietnam-war/cu-chi-tunnels-dangerous-underground-warzone.html)

388.

The "Black Tom explosion" happened on July 30th, 1916, when German saboteurs blew up a munitions depot in New York harbor. The explosion was the equivalent of an earthquake measuring between 5.0 and 5.5 on the Richter scale and caused permanent damage to the Statue of Liberty.

Reference: (https://en.wikipedia.org/wiki/Black_Tom_explosion)

389.

When Robert Ballard asked the Navy to fund his search for the Titanic, they told him to secretly survey two sunken U.S. nuclear subs first, to keep the USSR in the dark. After the covert mission was done, Ballard's team had only 12 days to find the Titanic.

Reference:
(https://en.wikipedia.org/wiki/Wreck_of_the_RMS_Titanic#Discovery)

390.

July 5th is the busiest day for animal shelters because so many pets run away in fear.

Reference: (http://dogtime.com/how-to/pet-safety/18007-july-5-busiest-day-of-the-year-for-u-dot-s-dot-animal-shelters)

391.

The Statue of Liberty's torch has been closed off to the public for more than 100 years due to damage sustained in World War I.

Reference: (https://www.amny.com/lifestyle/why-can-t-we-go-up-the-statue-of-liberty-s-torch-nycurious-1.7320932)

392.

Hedgehogs in cold climates hibernate over the winter. In warmer climates, such as deserts, they sleep through the heat and drought in a similar process called Aestivation. In more temperate areas they remain active all year.

Reference: (https://onekindplanet.org/animal/hedgehog-european/)

393.

Max Born, a German physicist who won the 1954 Nobel Prize in Physics and J. Robert Oppenheimer's doctoral advisor, is the grandfather of Olivia Newton-John, who played Sandy in "Grease."

Reference: (https://en.wikipedia.org/wiki/Max_Born)

394.

The Confederate army had a big problem with orgies, male prostitutes, and soldier's wives pretending to be new recruits to sleep with their husbands. Oddly, however, pornographic material has only been found on Union troops.

Reference: (https://oldtowncrier.com/2014/12/01/sex-and-the-civil-war/)

395.

Orca whales have very large and developed brains. They can communicate in different dialects, feel a wide range of emotions, and they have shown self-awareness.

Reference: (http://greymattersjournal.com/killer-whales-are-non-human-persons/)

396.

To prevent venereal disease among American World War I troops, the Chamberlain-Kahn Act was passed allowing the government to detain, examine, and quarantine U.S. women suspected of an STD. Common treatments included forced injections of mercury or compounds of arsenic.

Reference: (http://harvardjlg.com/wp-content/uploads/2015/06/38.2-Stern-The-Long-American-Plan.pdf)

397.

Homo sapiens had a conservation status of "Least Concern" as they are, "adaptable, currently increasing, and have no major threats."

Reference: (http://www.iucnredlist.org/details/136584/0)

398.

Traffic is so bad in Bangkok that the Thai Traffic Police has a unit of officers trained in basic midwifery in order to assist deliveries which do not reach the hospital in time.

Reference: (https://en.wikipedia.org/wiki/Transport_in_Bangkok)

399.

There are drive-thru funerals in Japan for those in a crunch for time.

Reference: (https://www.vice.com/en_ca/article/bj3qy5/drive-thru-funerals-are-now-a-thing-in-japan)

400.

Cloud iridescence is when the Sun scatters light from things like ice crystals in cirrus clouds into your eyes, therefore, making a rainbow color.

Reference: (https://en.wikipedia.org/wiki/Cloud_iridescence)

401.

The word "spider" in the automotive industry has its roots in the 1800s horse drawn carriages. These carriages, also called Phaetons, came in various shapes and sizes and the light weight ones, which because of its small and high body and large thin spoke wheels looked like a "spider."

Reference: (https://www.roadandtrack.com/car-culture/a20685360/why-convertibles-are-called-spiders/)

402.

Debbie Harry was 33 when "Blondie" first became successful.

Reference: (https://en.wikipedia.org/wiki/Debbie_Harry)

403.

President John Adams and his Vice President Thomas Jefferson died on the same day, July 4th, 1826.

Reference: (https://www.history.com/news/july-4-two-presidents-died-same-day-coincidence)

404.

The 1995 Bojinka plot was a plan to assassinate the pope, bomb 11 U.S.-Asia airliners, and fly a plane into the CIA headquarters. It was foiled after an accidental fire drew suspicion from Filipino police. It was financed by Bin Laden and 9/11 is considered to be a 2nd attempt at a similar attack.

Reference: (https://en.wikipedia.org/wiki/Bojinka_plot)

405.

Winston Churchill received his first standing ovation in Parliament after explaining why the British had destroyed the French Fleet.

Reference: (https://ww2db.com/person_bio.php?person_id=89)

406.

The U.S. has twice the GDP of every other country in North America, Central America, South America and the Caribbean combined.

Reference:
(https://en.wikipedia.org/wiki/List_of_countries_by_GDP_(nominal)
)

407.

Betty Shabazz, wife of civil rights advocate Malcolm X, died from severe burn wounds when her grandson, aged 12, accidentally burned down her apartment in 1997.

Reference: (https://en.wikipedia.org/wiki/Betty_Shabazz)

408.

There is an organization dedicated to smuggling documentaries, American TV shows, and South Korean pop culture into North Korea through USB drives and SD cards.

Reference: (https://www.wired.com/2015/03/heres-activists-smuggle-friends-north-korea/)

409.

Nanodiamonds or hyperdiamonds are about 80% tougher than ordinary diamonds.

Reference:
(https://en.wikipedia.org/wiki/Aggregated_diamond_nanorod)

410.

Tony Barrow, known for playing mobster Larry Barese in "The Sopranos", was arrested in 2011 for ordering the maiming of a man owing money to a loan shark. One of his partners in crime was a Gambino mob member.

Reference: (https://en.wikipedia.org/wiki/Tony_Darrow)

411.

Tequila is made from steamed agave, whereas Mezcal is cooked in wood-filled earthen pits, hence the smokey flavor.

Reference: (https://www.foodandwine.com/cocktails-spirits/differences-between-tequila-mezcal)

412.

The song "YMCA" by Village People is implicitly understood as celebrating the YMCA's reputation as a popular cruising and hookup spot for gay men.

Reference: (https://en.wikipedia.org/wiki/Y.M.C.A._(song))

413.

The Maldives highest point is only about 2.4 meters, or 8 feet tall. This means some people are literally taller than the entire country of the Maldives.

Reference: (https://www.nationalgeographic.com/travel/digital-nomad/2013/11/05/climbing-the-highest-point-in-the-maldives/)

414.

In 1918, at the request of President Woodrow Wilson, Henry Ford ran for the U.S. Senate in Michigan. Ford did not actively campaign, and he only lost to his opponent, Truman Newberry, former Secretary of the Navy, by 2,200 votes.

Reference: (https://www.thehenryford.org/collections-and-research/digital-collections/artifact/256288/#slide=gs_243404)

415.

The September, 2012, raid on Camp Bastion was the first time in over 70 years Marine pilots and mechanics from VMA-211 fought as infantry, the last time being during the Japanese attack on Wake Island.

Reference: (https://en.wikipedia.org/wiki/September_2012_raid_on_Camp_Bastion#The_raid)

416.

While trapped in a Chilean mine for 69 days, Edison Peña ran several miles a day underground. He has since ran in the New York Marathon and Tokyo Marathon.

Reference:
(http://content.time.com/time/photogallery/0,29307,2036984_22187 57,00.html)

417.

An Israeli Mossad agent by the name Eli Cohen infiltrated the government of Syria and convinced them to plant trees, which was later used by the Israelis as targeting markers in the 6 day war.

Reference:
(https://en.wikipedia.org/wiki/Eli_Cohen#Intelligence_collected)

418.

The first African-American billionaire was Robert Johnson, the founder of BET.

Reference: (https://www.biography.com/people/robert-l-johnson-41036)

419.

The original name of the Mona Lisa was Monna Lisa, but a spelling mistake made it the Mona Lisa. In Italian, Monna means Madonna, which means "My lady".

Reference:
(http://www.softschools.com/facts/history/mona_lisa_facts/2140/)

420.

Americans sought comfort TV after 9/11 and watched so much Food Network that the station had to restructure itself to appeal to a general audience. This led to the creation and subsequent rise of reality cooking shows like "Chopped" and "Iron Chef USA."

Reference: (https://youtu.be/T1-k7VYwsHg?t=720)

421.

The name of the Monopoly man is Rich Uncle Pennybags.

Reference: (http://wikipedia.org/wiki/Rich_Uncle_Pennybags)

422.

The name "Columbia" was used by some colonists to refer to the United States and was even visualized as a female national personification of America. During the independence, no serious consideration was given to using the name Columbia as an official name for the U.S.

Reference:
(https://en.wikipedia.org/wiki/Columbia_(name)#Personification)

423.

The Treskilling Yellow, a Swedish postage stamp, is one of the rarest stamps in the whole world. Because of how rare it is, it is to be worth more than $3.14 million U.S. dollars.

Reference: (http://www.china.org.cn/top10/2012-04/27/content_25224963_13.htm)

424.

The flag on the Moon was bought from a nearby Sears.

Reference: (https://www.history.nasa.gov/alsj/ApolloFlags-Condition.html)

425.

The Star Spangled Banner borrowed its tune from "To Anacreon in Heaven", a British drinking song hailing the praises of an Ancient Greek poet famous for loving wine and writing erotic poetry.

Reference:
(http://www.questseans.com/yesterwierd/2018/6/20/where-did-the-star-spangled-banner-come-from)

426.

On March 5th, 1973, a couple dozen people headed out to a farm in Ossineke, Michigan, to witness the burial of an estimated 30,000 frozen, family-size mushroom pizzas.

Reference: (https://www.atlasobscura.com/articles/michigan-pizza-funeral)

427.

As well as preparing for TV Pickups, the National Grid also prepares for synchronized switch offs. In one instance, they argued against a mass switch-off as it would have resulted in highly unpredictable demands for power and would have resulted in producing more carbon dioxide than it saved.

Reference: (https://en.wikipedia.org/wiki/TV_pickup#Records)

428.

There is an international hide and seek competition in a ghost town in Italy.

Reference:
(https://en.wikipedia.org/wiki/Hide_and_Seek_World_Championship)

429.

Even though Hitler was the pioneer of "The Final Solution", which was implemented to exterminate the Jewish race, he never personally visited a single death camp.

Reference: (http://www.warhistoryonline.com/war-articles/20-mind-boggling-hitler-facts.html/3)

430.

WWE had a Canadian Main-title holder and Canadian midcard title holder. Now, NJPW has a Canadian Main-title and midcard title holder. In both cases, the midcard title holder was Chris Jericho.

Reference: (https://en.wikipedia.org/wiki/Chris_Jericho)

431.

During this solar minimum, radiation from deep space is worsening and can cause cardiac arrhythmias in the general population.

Reference: (https://spaceweatherarchive.com/2018/03/05/the-worsening-cosmic-ray-situation/)

432.

The female of the Bluehead wrasse fish can change sex and become a male.

Reference: (https://en.wikipedia.org/wiki/Bluehead_wrasse)

433.

Before the Watergate Scandal, the Teapot Dome Scandal was regarded as the most sensational example of high-level corruption in the history of U.S. politics.

Reference: (https://www.history.com/topics/teapot-dome-scandal)

434.

Johnny Cash wrote a personal letter to U.S. President Gerald Ford regarding his pardon of Richard Nixon for crimes he may have committed.

Reference: (https://www.docsteach.org/documents/document/cash-ford-pardons)

435.

Before 1982, the approval of the British Parliament was required to change Canada's Constitution.

Reference:
(https://en.wikipedia.org/wiki/Amendments_to_the_Constitution_of_Canada)

436.

A rain drop travels about 14 miles per hour and takes about two minutes to fall to the ground coming from your average cloud at 2,500 feet.

Reference:
(https://www.metoffice.gov.uk/learning/precipitation/rain/facts-about-rain)

437.

Demetri Martin, while studying at Yale, submitted a 224 word palindromic poem for a fractal geometry course project.

Reference:(https://users.math.yale.edu/public_html/People/frame/Fractals/Panorama/Literature/Martin/MartinPalindrome.html)

438.

The record for missing penalties in a soccer game by one player goes to Martín Palermo, who missed 3 for Argentina against Colombia in Copa América 1999. In FIFAWorld Cup 2010, he scored his first ever World Cup goal, making him the oldest Argentine national footballer to score in a World Cup match.

Reference:
(https://en.wikipedia.org/wiki/Mart%C3%ADn_Palermo#International_career)

439.

Endocannibalism is a practice of eating the flesh of a human being from the same community, usually after they have died.

Reference: (https://en.wikipedia.org/wiki/Endocannibalism)

440.

Lamar Gant, an IPF powerlifter who deadlifted 661 pounds (300 kilograms) at 132 pounds (60 kilograms) becoming the first human in history to deadlift 5 times their bodyweight. He accomplished this despite having severe scoliosis.

Reference: (https://en.wikipedia.org/wiki/Lamar_Gant)

441.

Star Trek's Warp Speed "warp factor 1" means travelling at 1 times the speed of light. Once in The Next Generation, Riker claims that the Enterprise would need around 20 minutes for a 300 billion kilometer flight at Warp 9. Therefore, Warp Factor 9 corresponds to a speed of 900 billion kilometers per hour.

Reference: (http://memory-alpha.wikia.com/wiki/Warp_drive)

442.

Radium tablets were once used to treat rheumatism and were believed to enhance endurance.

Reference:
(https://www.orau.org/ptp/collection/quackcures/arium.htm)

443.

An angry guy has hacked the HBO signal in 1986 to complain about the price of his monthly payment.

Reference: (https://www.networkworld.com/article/2229101/security/security-captain-midnight-no-regrets-about-jamming-hbo-back-in-86.html)

444.

Lawnmower blades create an upward airflow as they spin, lifting the grass and allowing for a better cut.

Reference: (https://en.wikipedia.org/wiki/Mower_blade)

445.

Sinatra had fan clubs with names such as the Slaves of Sinatra, the Sighing Society of Sinatra, Swooners, the Flatbush Girls Who Would Lay Down Their Lives for Frank Sinatra, and the Frank Sinatra Fan and Mahjong Club.

Reference: (https://www.nytimes.com/2010/11/01/books/excerpt-frank.html)

446.

The largest contingent of the KKK west of the Mississippi was 35,000 strong and it was in Oregon.

Reference: (http://www.wweek.com/arts/2017/08/17/oregon-was-once-ku-ku-for-the-klan/)

447.

In the U.K., banks share your exact monthly deposits, down to the pound, with 3rd parties.

Reference: (https://www.telegraph.co.uk/personal-banking/current-accounts/how-your-bank-spies-on-your-exact-monthly-income---and-shares-it/)

448.

For 9 years, the U.S. had a justice surnamed Black while having another justice surnamed White.

Reference:(https://en.wikipedia.org/wiki/List_of_Justices_of_the_Supreme_Court_of_the_United_States#All_justices_of_the_Supreme_Court)

449.

Starting in 1902, Quaker Oats oatmeal boxes included a coupon redeemable for a legal deed to a tiny plot of land in Milford, Connecticut that were known as "Oatmeal Lots." In 1955, the company put actual deeds to land in the Klondike in its Puffed Wheat and Puffed Rice cereal boxes.

Reference: (https://www.ctpost.com/local/article/Oatmeal-lots-gave-officials-indigestion-687006.php)

450.

Michael Caine claims that his Cockney accent would have prevented a British director from casting him as an officer in the 1964 film "Zulu." The film was directed by an American.

Reference: (https://www.cbsnews.com/news/60-minutes-michael-caine-youth-lesley-stahl/)

451.

Jethro Tull, not heavy metal band, won the first Hard Rock and Heavy Metal Grammy award. The decision was so lampooned that they split the award into separate Hard Rock and Heavy Metal categories for all future awards.

Reference: (https://www.rollingstone.com/music/music-news/metallicas-lars-ulrich-recalls-f-ed-up-1989-grammy-loss-179972/)

452.

Charlie Chaplin was married 4 times and had 11 children, 8 of whom with his 4th wife.

Reference:
(https://en.wikipedia.org/wiki/Charlie_Chaplin#Legal_troubles_and_Oona_O'Neill)

453.

14 years ago, a flock of Yorkshire sheep learnt to roll over 3 meter long cattle grids in order to eat the plants in the local gardens and graze on the village Bowling Green.

Reference: (http://news.bbc.co.uk/1/hi/uk/3938591.stm)

454.

When Prince Charles was invested as the Prince of Wales in 1969, the orb on top of his investiture coronet was gold plated over a ping-pong ball. The coronet still contains the ping pong ball.

Reference:
(https://www.1066.co.nz/Mosaic%20DVD/library/The%20Crown%20Jewels.pdf)

455.

Radioactive substances were once a health craze.

Reference: (https://www.popsci.com/scitech/article/2004-08/healthy-glow-drink-radiation#page-4)

456.

In 2000, according to a World Bank estimate, khat, a drug, accounted for 30% of Yemen's economy.

Reference:
(https://en.wikipedia.org/wiki/Khat#Cultivation_and_uses)

457.

The "healthiest hearts in the world" were found in a Bolivian forest people, who get 72% of their energy from carbohydrates, which is the exact opposite to many recent suggestions that carbohydrates are unhealthy.

Reference: (https://www.bbc.co.uk/news/health-39292389)

458.

After a year-long petition with the NFL, Mike Nolan received permission to wear a dress suit designed by Reebok on the sidelines of a game.

Reference: (http://www.espn.com/nfl/news/story?id=2663580)

459.

July 2, 1776, was the day when the Continental Congress actually voted for independence, not July 4. John Adams even wrote to his wife Abigail that, "The Second Day of July 1776, will be the most memorable Epocha, in the History of America", and would be marked with fireworks and celebrations.

Reference: (https://www.nbcnews.com/news/us-news/fourth-july-traditions-link-americans-countrys-past-v19223660)

460.

The fictional character Steve Rogers, Captain America, was born on the 4th of July.

Reference: (http://comicbook.com/2015/07/04/happy-birthday-steve-rogers-a-k-a-captain-america-/)

461.

In 1998, Joe Pesci released a rap single called "Wise Guy."

Reference: (https://www.youtube.com/watch?v=QrrkPHPwVfo)

462.

The Worcester Worcesters, an MLB team that existed in the National League from 1880 to 1882, folded because the town in which it was based, Worcester, Massachusetts, was deemed too small for a professional sports team. Their spot was taken by the Philadelphia Phillies.

Reference: (https://en.wikipedia.org/wiki/Worcester_Worcesters)

463.

On average, every 2 minutes a person dies in a car crash. In the U.S. alone, about every 15 minutes one person dies on the road.

Reference: (http://asirt.org/Initiatives/Informing-Road-Users/Road-Safety-Facts/Road-Crash-Statistics)

464.

The Foundation series by Issac Asimov won the Hugo Award for the best all-time series in 1966. The Lord of the Rings was runner up.

Reference: (http://www.nesfa.org/data/LL/Hugos/hugos1966.html)

465.

Stars are added to the American flag for new states on July 4th.

Reference: (https://www.si.edu/spotlight/flag-day/flag-facts)

466.

Mark Hamill played Mozart in the play "Amadeus." When a movie adaptation of the play was being developed, Mark Hamill wanted to audition to play Mozart again. Director Miloš Forman refused to let

Hamill even audition for the part because he didn't think Luke Skywalker should be playing the Mozart.

Reference: (https://www.praguereporter.com/home/2017/12/8/luke-skywalker-almost-became-mozart-in-milo-formans-amadeus)

467.

Lock and dam 52 on the Ohio River is the busiest in the U.S. with roughly 135 million tons of cargo passing every year. It's in serious need of repair and the locks should have been replaced in 1988 and has been in construction since 1998 with an estimated completion of 2024.

Reference:
(https://en.wikipedia.org/wiki/Lock_and_Dam_Number_52)

468.

The writer of the Chili's "Baby Back Ribs" jingle wrote it in 5 minutes, had the songwriting rights taken away from him, and has never had baby back ribs from Chili's.

Reference: (https://munchies.vice.com/en_us/article/ypx4dy/the-inventor-of-the-chilis-baby-back-ribs-song-has-never-eaten-their-ribs)

469.

The pilot episode of "Gilligan's Island" theme song was composed by none other than John Williams.

Reference:
(https://en.wikipedia.org/wiki/Gilligan%27s_Island#Theme_song)

470.

The Anna hummingbird, when adjusted for body size, is the world's fastest bird. It travels an average of 385 times its size per second, compared to the peregrine falcon's 200. It can also pull up to 10g's during maneuvers.

Reference:
(https://news.nationalgeographic.com/news/2009/06/090612-fastest-flying-bird.html)

471.

In the 1990's, the CIA conducted research on "Remote Viewing" and "Astral Projection" under Project Stargate.

Reference: (https://www.cia.gov/library/readingroom/docs/CIA-RDP96-00789R003300210001-2.pdf)

472.

A Scottish woman named Maggie Dickson, was sentenced to execution by hanging on September 2nd, 1724. She survived the hanging and climbed out of her coffin as it was being transported. The courts ruled she was a free woman as the punishment had been carried out.

Reference:
(https://www.undiscoveredscotland.co.uk/usbiography/d/maggiedickson.html)

473.

In 1978, U.S. Congress' House Select Committee on Assassinations officially concluded that the three autopsy surgeons who examined John F. Kennedy's body together misidentified the anatomic location of a gunshot wound in the head.

Reference: (https://history-matters.com/archive/jfk/hsca/reportvols/vol7/html/HSCA_Vol7_0062b.htm)

474.

A "nail house" is a home whose resident refuses to leave in order to make way for new construction. In China, this has led to some almost sculpture-like creations.

Reference: (https://io9.gizmodo.com/unbelievable-nail-houses-around-the-world-892781747)

475.

Sigiriya in Sri Lanka is a massive column of rock where a fortress once stood.

Reference: (https://en.wikipedia.org/wiki/Sigiriya)

476.

Banksy was the goalkeeper for the Easton Cowboys and Cowgirls football team in the 1990s, and toured with the club to Mexico in 2001. While there, he painted a number of murals in the community.

Reference: (https://en.wikipedia.org/wiki/Banksy#cite_ref-bbc_onyangaomara_2012_17-0)

477.

In 1966, Kenneth McDuff murdered three people and was sentenced to death. His sentence was later commuted to life, and he was paroled in 1989. He went on to murder at least four more people, was caught in 1992, once again sentenced to death, and executed in 1998.

Reference: (https://en.wikipedia.org/wiki/Kenneth_McDuff)

478.

Bulletproof glass can be manufactured to be bulletproof one way, but allow you to shoot through it the other way.

Reference: (https://www.tssbulletproof.com/blog/one-way-ballistic-glass/)

479.

Maverick is a term, usually referring to cattle, for an animal that does not carry a brand. Other U.S. terms for unbranded cattle include slick, hairy dick, and, in Spanish-speaking areas of the Southwest, orejano.

Reference: (https://en.wikipedia.org/wiki/Maverick_(animal))

480.

In 1942, the U.S. War Department borrowed 14,000 tons of Government silver to aid in the production of enough enriched uranium to make a nuclear weapon.

Reference: (https://www.americanscientist.org/article/from-treasury-vault-to-the-manhattan-project)

481.

It's not illegal to chew gum in Singapore, unlike what most people believe. It is, however, illegal to import large quantities of gum except nicotine and dental gum.

Reference: (http://thesmartlocal.com/read/rumours-about-singapore)

482.

There are operating triple-expansion steam engines in existence and the largest is in the U.K.

Reference: (https://www.youtube.com/watch?v=FuHJBIMj_rs)

483.

Dylan Sprouse, Zack from the "Suite Life," is now a master brewer of mead. He also practices Germanic-Paganism which inspires his brewing.

Reference: (http://bedfordandbowery.com/2017/01/prepare-to-get-buzzed-with-a-former-child-star-at-all-wise-meadery/)

484.

1 gram of activated charcoal has approximately 1,000 square meters of surface area.

Reference: (https://www.sciencedirect.com/topics/pharmacology-toxicology-and-pharmaceutical-science/activated-carbon)

485.

Bernie Taupin, who is most famous for writing songs for Elton John, also wrote "We Built This City".

Reference: (https://en.wikipedia.org/wiki/We_Built_This_Cit)

486.

Thomas Jefferson preferred to communicate through writing so he did not give the annual State of the Union address. Instead, he had a representative do it for him. This became a tradition that lasted until Woodrow Wilson decided to make his own speech. It's been that way ever since.

Reference:
(https://en.wikipedia.org/wiki/Thomas_Jefferson#Linguistics)

487.

1 in 3 prescriptions go unfilled, according to a study in Quebec, even though 50% of citizens have some provincial drug coverage.

Reference: (https://www.aafp.org/news/health-of-the-public/20140428nonadherencestudy.html)

488.

Canada is the Iroquois word for land. Canada is Land, founded alongside Newfoundland.

Reference: (https://en.wikipedia.org/wiki/Name_of_Canada)

489.

Before cola became widespread, hamburgers were typically served with coffee.

Reference:
(https://en.wikipedia.org/wiki/History_of_the_hamburger)

490.

A 15 year old hacker caused a 21 day shutdown of NASA computers supporting the International Space Station and Pentagon weapon system. He also hacked the Defense Threat Reduction Agency, whose mission is to reduce threats from nuclear, biological, chemical, conventional and special weapons.

Reference:
(https://abcnews.go.com/Technology/story?id=119423&page=1)

491.

Free-ranging cats kill billions of birds annually in the U.S. They are the #1 anthropogenic cause of death for birds.

Reference:
(https://www.annualreviews.org/doi/full/10.1146/annurev-ecolsys-112414-054133)

492.

Wombats can run at a speed of 40 kilometers per hour, 3 kilometers per hour faster than Usain Bolt's average running speed during his world record. They also make cubic dung, which is thought to be so they can mark their territory without the dung rolling away.

Reference: (https://en.wikipedia.org/wiki/Wombat)

493.

In 2015, the town of Collecchio in Italy passed a law requiring the use of "silent fireworks" to help reduce stress on veterans, pets, children, and wildlife. While not completely silent, they are much quieter than traditional fireworks and can be more colorful.

Reference: (https://www.nytimes.com/2016/07/01/science/july-4-fireworks-quiet.html)

494.

According to a 2009 study by the University of Westminster, the less religious people are, the more likely they are to believe in UFOs, intelligent aliens monitoring the lives of humans, and related conspiracies about a government cover-up of these phenomena.

Reference:
(https://www.nytimes.com/2017/07/21/opinion/sunday/dont-believe-in-god-maybe-youll-try-ufos.html)

495.

Not only has the British Royal Navy named a ship the HMS Cockchafer, but that they have used the name at least 4 times. Also, a cockchafer is a type of insect.

Reference:
(https://en.wikipedia.org/wiki/HMS_Cockchafer_%281915%29)

496.

The record for the most titles in the European Basketball Championship is still held by the Soviet Union.

Reference: (https://en.wikipedia.org/wiki/EuroBasket)

497.

The United States Air Force F-22A Raptor stealth fighter jet's canopy is resistant to chemical, biological and environmental agents, and has been successfully tested to withstand the impact of a four-pound bird at 350 knots. It also protects the pilot from lightning strikes.

Reference:
(https://www.globalsecurity.org/military/systems/aircraft/f-22-cockpit.htm)

498.

Benjamin Franklin introduced the colonies to kitesurfing.

Reference: (http://mentalfloss.com/article/71431/time-ben-franklin-casually-invented-form-kitesurfing)

499.

Silvestre Herrera, a Mexican citizen and volunteer U.S. soldier during World War II, received the Medal of Honor. He charged an enemy stronghold through a minefield, blowing off both of his feet. He continued fighting on his knees, pinning down the enemy and allowing his squad to capture it.

Reference: (https://en.wikipedia.org/wiki/Silvestre_S._Herrera)

500.

At 3,987 miles, the U.S.-Canada border, excluding Alaska, is twice as long as the U.S.-Mexico border.

Reference:(https://www2.census.gov/library/publications/2010/compendia/statab/130ed/tables/11s0359.pdf)

501.

The U.S. flag is considered a living thing by law.

Reference: (https://www.law.cornell.edu/uscode/text/4/8)

502.

Dogs can suffer from PTSD.

Reference: (https://wagwalking.com/condition/post-traumatic-stress-disorder)

503.

Two trapped miners once asked for an iPod with The Foo Fighters music on it to keep their spirits up. After hearing this, Dave Grohl wrote a note saying, "I want you to know that when you come home, there's two tickets to any Foos show, anywhere, and two cold beers waiting for you".

Reference: (https://www.stereoboard.com/content/view/181/9)

504.

A woman named Carol Carr killed her two adult sons in a nursing home after she couldn't see them suffer from Huntington's disease anymore.

Reference: (https://en.wikipedia.org/wiki/Carol_Carr)

505.

Serotonin, a chemical produced by nerve cells, helps us keep calm, happy and emotionally stable. Its deficiency results in depression and anxiety. Chocolate lovers are usually happy as dark chocolates and nuts help increase serotonin.

Reference: (https://www.healthline.com/health/mental-health/serotonin#serotonin-boosters)

506.

In 2014, the world's largest earwig, which was 8 centimeters or a little over 3 inches long, was declared extinct.

Reference: (http://www.bbc.com/earth/story/20141117-giant-earwig-declared-extinct)

507.

Mary from "Mary had a little Lamb" was a real girl; Mary Sawyer from Sudbury, Massachusetts.

Reference:
(https://en.wikipedia.org/wiki/Mary_Had_a_Little_Lamb)

508.

As a young man, C.S. Lewis, Christian theologian and author of the Chronicles of Narnia, was keen on sadomasochism, read the works of de Sade, and once begged partygoers to let him beat them with a whip.

Reference: (http://religion.blogs.cnn.com/2013/12/01/the-c-s-lewis-you-never-knew/comment-page-1/)

509.

On July 4th, 1852, Frederick Douglass was asked to give a speech about Independence. He got real angry, saying it was a sham, since slaves had no independence. He said, "This Fourth of July is yours, not mine. You may rejoice, I must mourn."

Reference: (http://www.pbs.org/wgbh/aia/part4/4h2927.html)

510.

Swiss banks bought gold and stolen paintings from Nazi Germany during World War II.

Reference: (https://en.wikipedia.org/wiki/Nazi_gold)

511.

Composer Giuseppe Tartini had a dream in which the Devil presented himself to him. Tartini gave the Devil a violin and the Devil played a solo so beautiful it surpassed anything he's ever heard in his life. When Tartini awoke he tried to recreate the piece and composed the "Devils Trill Sonata."

Reference: (https://www.primephonic.com/the-music-of-dreams-how-tartini-composed-his-famous-devils-trill-sonata)

512.

"Kodachrome" by Paul Simon was banned from BBC Radio because it mentions a brand name.

Reference: (http://www.songfacts.com/detail.php?id=1216)

513.

Kevin Smith, director of "Dogma," attended a protest of the movie undisguised and spoke against it.

Reference: (http://legendsrevealed.com/entertainment/2012/09/27/did-kevin-smith-once-picket-his-own-film/)

514.

English actor Jake Weber, who played Alison Dubois' husband on "Medium" and shock jock Brett O'Keefe on "Homeland," was used by his father as a drug mule to bring cocaine to Mick and Bianca Jagger's wedding when he was only 8 years old.

Reference: (https://en.wikipedia.org/wiki/Jake_Weber)

515.

People used to say, "The United States of America are..." instead of "is"; it only changed after the Civil War.

Reference: (https://www.visualthesaurus.com/cm/wordroutes/the-united-states-is-or-are/)

516.

Foxes not only have whiskers on their faces, they have whiskers on their legs as well to help them navigate around.

Reference: (https://onekindplanet.org/animal/fox-red/)

517.

George Lincoln Rockwell, founder of the American Nazi Party, was friends with Elijah Muhammad, leader of the Nation of Islam, due in part to their shared hatred of Jews and desire for racial segregation.

Reference: (https://www.vice.com/en_us/article/dpwamv/when-malcolm-x-met-the-nazis-0000620-v22n4)

518.

The Vatican City is the country that drinks the most wine per capita at 74 liters per citizen, per year.

Reference: (https://www.huffingtonpost.co.uk/2014/02/25/vatican-wine_n_4851410.html)

519.

Terrence Malick came up with the ending for "Goodwill Hunting."

Reference: (http://www.slashfilm.com/trivia-terrence-malick-gave-good-hunting/)

520.

Redheads with blue eyes, the rarest color combination of all for human beings, aren't actually going extinct.

Reference: (https://pursuit.unimelb.edu.au/articles/are-redheads-with-blue-eyes-really-going-extinct?utm_source=twiter&utm_medium=social&utm_content=story)

521.

Rabbits have good hearing, and sight, and an excellent sense of smell. They detect predators quickly, and then signal others by thumping their hind legs before seeking the shelter of the burrow.

Reference: (https://onekindplanet.org/animal/rabbit/)

522.

The Soviet Union successfully used horse cavalry against the Nazis during World War II. They were often grouped together with fast moving tanks to push deep into enemy territory once a breakthrough in the front had been achieved.

Reference:
(https://en.wikipedia.org/wiki/Cavalry_mechanized_group)

523.

Anne Ramsey, along with her husband, once owned, operated and even named the Theater Of The Living Arts in Philadelphia. The building is now a popular concert venue.

Reference: (http://cinematreasures.org/theaters/13824)

524.

"Hail to the Chief", the U.S. Presidential theme, has lyrics.

Reference: (http://www.metrolyrics.com/hail-to-the-chief-lyrics-traditional.html)

525.

The first winnowing machine for corn, which used fans to separate grain from chaff, was condemned by Presbyterian ministers because wind was a thing specially made by God and an artificial wind was an attempt to usurp what belonged to God alone.

Reference:
(https://en.wikipedia.org/wiki/Winnowing#Mechanization_of_the_pr
[ocess](https://en.wikipedia.org/wiki/Winnowing#Mechanization_of_the_process))

526.

Actor Dennis Hopper was a huge fan of the band Killer Pussy, best known for their single "Teenage Enema Nurses in Bondage." Hopper painted a portrait of lead singer Lucy LaMode, which was displayed prominently on the Sarah Jessica Parker sitcom "Square Pegs."

Reference: ([http://www.phoenixnewtimes.com/music/killer-pussy-](http://www.phoenixnewtimes.com/music/killer-pussy-old-school-phoenix-punk-parodists-gather-for-30th-anniversary-reunion-6432716)
[old-school-phoenix-punk-parodists-gather-for-30th-anniversary-](http://www.phoenixnewtimes.com/music/killer-pussy-old-school-phoenix-punk-parodists-gather-for-30th-anniversary-reunion-6432716)
[reunion-6432716](http://www.phoenixnewtimes.com/music/killer-pussy-old-school-phoenix-punk-parodists-gather-for-30th-anniversary-reunion-6432716))

527.

Lillian Virginia Mountweazel was a woman famous for being fake. She appears in the 1975 New Columbia Encyclopedia as a photographer famous for pictures of rural American mailboxes until dying in an explosion while on assignment, but in reality she's only a copyright trap to detect plagiarism.

Reference: ([https://www.newyorker.com/magazine/2005/08/29/not-](https://www.newyorker.com/magazine/2005/08/29/not-a-word)
[a-word](https://www.newyorker.com/magazine/2005/08/29/not-a-word))

528.

The phrase "Eat healthy" is incorrect grammar. The correct form is "Eat healthily".

Reference: ([https://jakubmarian.com/eat-healthily-vs-eat-healthy-in-](https://jakubmarian.com/eat-healthily-vs-eat-healthy-in-english/)
[english/](https://jakubmarian.com/eat-healthily-vs-eat-healthy-in-english/))

529.

Despite conventional wisdom, the #1 best treatment for jellyfish or man o' war stings is vinegar and hot water.

Reference: (https://gizmodo.com/science-reveals-the-right-way-to-treat-a-man-o-war-jel-1794880485)

530.

The British once built a 1,100-mile 12 by 14 feet hedge through the middle of India to impose a high salt tax on the people living on one side of the line.

Reference: (https://www.atlasobscura.com/articles/colonial-india-british-hedge-salt-tax)

531.

Coca-Cola's secret ingredients used to be cocaine and caffeine from the coca leaf and the kola nut.

Reference: (https://forgottenhistoryblog.com/coca-colas-secret-ingredient-used-to-be-cocaine/)

532.

Sheep can remember the faces of 50 other sheep for at least two years.

Reference: (https://onekindplanet.org/animal-behaviour/emotions/emotions-in-sheep/)

533.

The original "Toy Story 3" screenplay was about Buzz Lightyear malfunctioning, getting recalled, and shipped back to Taiwan. The other toys went there to save him, while Buzz meets other recalled toys.

Reference:
(http://disney.wikia.com/wiki/Toy_Story_3_(Circle_7_Screenplay))

534.

Geckos climb walls by using Van Der Waals forces.

Reference: (https://youtu.be/gzm7yD-JuyM?t=1m30s)

535.

The U.K. government didn't apologize for their treating of Alan Turing until 2009, 55 years after his suicide. He died when he was 41.

Reference: (https://learnodo-newtonic.com/alan-turing-facts)

536.

The Shell Grotto is a mysterious underground chamber discovered in a back garden in the South East of England during the Victorian era. Buried a few feet underground, it was excavated and found to contain a myriad of religious symbols from around the world. Its origins remain a mystery.

Reference: (https://en.wikipedia.org/wiki/Shell_Grotto,_Margate)

537.

Legal separation of the Thirteen Colonies from Great Britain actually occurred on July 2nd, 1776, when the Second Continental Congress voted to approve a resolution of independence declaring the United States independent from Great Britain's rule.

Reference:
(https://en.wikipedia.org/wiki/Independence_Day_(United_States)?repost)

538.

It was revealed on PBS' "Finding Your Roots," that actress Kyra Sedgwick and her husband Kevin Bacon are actually distant cousins.

Reference: (http://observer.com/2017/08/kyra-sedgwick-kevin-bacon-cousins-info-details/)

539.

Although being tarred and feathered was depicted as barbaric and caused great stress to the victim, death rarely, if ever, followed, as pine tar is stored at half the temperature than the tar used for paving modern day roads.

Reference: (https://allthingsliberty.com/2013/12/5-myths-tarring-feathering/)

540.

Bruce Willis' world-famous phrase "Yippee-ki-yay, motherfucker" in the "Die Hard" films is translated to "Yippee-Ya-Yeah, Schweinebacke" in the German version, which is named "Stirb langsam", or "Die slowly."

Reference: (https://www.youtube.com/watch?v=qYakukN8va8)

541.

Chinese Drywall, used in the U.S. in the mid-2000s, was so widely used and had so much sulfuric compound off-gassing, that it has destroyed the copper components in houses across the U.S.

Reference: (https://en.wikipedia.org/wiki/Chinese_drywall)

542.

Nail polish has been around for 5000 years.

Reference: (https://en.wikipedia.org/wiki/Nail_polish)

543.

The 1980s group Quarterflash was noteworthy for having a lead singer who played the saxophone. Their 1981 song "Harden My Heart" was their most successful. It was originally recorded under the band's old name, Seafood Mama.

Reference: (https://en.wikipedia.org/wiki/Quarterflash)

544.

Both Hugh Jackman and Patrick Stewart have urinated in bottles while stuck in traffic.

Reference: (https://youtu.be/SR6Hd9yDadc?t=5m15s)

545.

Firefighters recommend closing your bedroom door at night in case of fire. Closed doors have been shown to strongly limit heat and carbon monoxide in the bedroom. It could save your life.

Reference:
(https://www.youtube.com/watch?v=k_L8tW5xWnk&feature=youtu
.be)

546.

John Philip Sousa was paid only $35 for his second most popular work, "The Washington Post" March, while the publisher made a fortune. Of Sousa's earnings, $25 was for a piano arrangement, $5 for a band arrangement, and $5 for an orchestra arrangement.

Reference: (https://www.marineband.marines.mil/Audio-Resources/The-Complete-Marches-of-John-Philip-Sousa/The-Washington-Post-March/)

547.

The first commercial passenger airliner to be shot down by hostile forces was refurbished, returned to service, and later became the third commercial passenger airliner to be shot down by hostile forces.

Reference:(https://en.wikipedia.org/wiki/List_of_airliner_shootdown_incidents#Kweilin_Incident)

548.

The Jabba The Hutt puppet was 2,000 pounds, took 3 months to build, 3 men to operate and cost half a million dollars to construct.

Reference:
(https://en.wikipedia.org/wiki/Jabba_the_Hutt#Production_and_design)

549.

Roald Dahl, author of "Charlie and the Chocolate Factory" and "James and the Giant Peach", was also British spy known for gaining intelligence through sex.

Reference:(https://www.telegraph.co.uk/culture/books/biographyandmemoirreviews/7932042/Roald-Dahl-the-spy-who-loved-me.html)

550.

Forced Rhubarb grows so fast that you can hear it grow.

Reference: (https://boingboing.net/2018/04/13/ultra-fast-growing-rhubarb-mak.html)

551.

Fred Wiseman was the first person to deliver airmail in the world, only delivering a small handful of items.

Reference:
(http://www.airmailpioneers.org/content/milestone4.html)

552.

The Ottoman Empire lost a quarter of its population in World War I.

Reference:
(https://wikipedia.org/wiki/Ottoman_casualties_of_World_War_I)

553.

The name of Italy is at least 3000 years old and has a history that goes back to pre-Roman Italy. It initially referred to the tip of the Italian peninsula.

Reference: (https://en.wikipedia.org/wiki/Name_of_Italy)

554.

Irreducible complexity is the idea that certain biological systems cannot evolve by successive small modifications to pre-existing functional systems through natural selection. This idea is central to the creationist concept of intelligent design, but it is rejected by the scientific community.

Reference: (https://en.wikipedia.org/wiki/Irreducible_complexity)

555.

British Columbia was named to distinguish itself from "American Columbia", Columbia being the general namesake for The New World, deriving in honor of Christopher Columbus.

Reference: (https://en.wikipedia.org/wiki/British_Columbia)

556.

Liquid water can be supercooled to -55 degrees Fahrenheit, -48.3 degrees Celsius, 224.8 Kelvin, if the water is free from impurities or places where ice could form.

Reference: (https://en.wikipedia.org/wiki/Supercooling)

557.

Chile's National Stadium preserves a wooden bench section as a memorial. During the fascist dictatorship people would sit on those benches until being called up for their summary judgement and execution.

Reference:
(http://www.espn.com/soccer/club/chile/207/blog/post/2512371/chile-estadio-nacional-gate-8-sector-reminder-of-past)

558.

LEBRN, "LeBron", is and will forever be the designation for an airplane navigation marker above South Eastern Cleveland.

Reference:(https://www.cleveland.com/metro/index.ssf/2015/06/lebrn_a_fixture_in_sky_over_so.html)

559.

The first day of the week, for most, Sunday has been set aside as the "day of the Sun" since ancient Egyptian times in honor of the Sun-God, beginning with Ra.

Reference: (https://en.wikipedia.org/wiki/Sunday)

560.

Movie countdowns end with the number 2; the big 2 is called a 2-pop and it's a single frame span out through 2 seconds. The audio of the movie during that time is a single computer generated tone and it exists for audio synchronization when dealing with the sound separately.

Reference: (https://en.wikipedia.org/wiki/2-pop)

561.

The dancer who was Jennifer Beals' body double in "Flashdance" did the same thing for Snoopy in "Flashbeagle," the Peanuts parody.

Reference: (https://en.wikipedia.org/wiki/Marine_Jahan)

562.

In 1944, former president George H. W. Bush narrowly escaped being eaten by a Japanese general named Yoshio Tachibana.

Reference: (https://amp-businessinsider-com.cdn.ampproject.org/v/s/amp.businessinsider.com/how-george-hw-bush-avoided-being-eaten-by-cannibals-in-world-war-ii-2017-12?amp_js_v=a2&_gsa=1&usqp=mq331AQECAE4AQ%3D%3D#referrer=https://www.google.com&_tf=From%20%251%24s
)

563.

The Jules Rimet Trophy was permanently awarded to any country who won the FIFA World Cup three times. When Brazil achieved this after the 1970 World Cup, they were allowed to permanently keep it, however, it was stolen in 1983 and has never been fully recovered.

Reference:
(https://en.wikipedia.org/wiki/1970_FIFA_World_Cup_Final)

564.

Ants have passed the "Mirror Self-Recognition test."

Reference: (https://en.wikipedia.org/wiki/Mirror_test)

565.

Only 139 cars were manufactured in the U.S. during the entirety of its 4-year involvement in World War II due to the shift towards war production.

Reference:
(http://www.pbs.org/thewar/at_home_war_production.htm)

566.

Radio Yerevan jokes were very popular in the USSR and Combloc countries. They described the absurdity of everyday living under socialism. Jokes acted as a relatively safe way for the people to vent their frustration towards the authoritarian regime.

Reference: (https://en.wikipedia.org/wiki/Radio_Yerevan_jokes)

567.

The only book Stephen King has let go out of print is Rage, in which a kid shoots his teacher and holds his class hostage. While he doesn't think books, movies, or video games cause violence, he does think they could act as an outlet to commit violence through, and should be more responsible.

Reference: (https://www.youtube.com/watch?v=2TmFVtsu118)

568.

There is a city in China called "Hallstatt" whose core is modelled after the small Austrian city "Hallstatt."

Reference: (https://en.wikipedia.org/wiki/Hallstatt_(China))

569.

Castor, in the Gemini constellation, is actually a sextuple star system, with two binary pairs orbiting each other and a third pair orbiting slightly further away; all close enough to appear as a single point of light from Earth.

Reference:
(https://www.youtube.com/watch?v=bV3MrXwOU0k&feature=youtu.be)

570.

For the 1942 Rose Bowl, played weeks after Pearl Harbor, the Oregon State Beavers only traveled with 31 players because their 32nd player, Chiaki "Jack" Yoshihara, was not permitted to go more than 35 miles from his home due to the new executive order.

Reference:(https://en.wikipedia.org/wiki/1942_Rose_Bowl#Venue_change_to_Durham,_North_Carolina)

571.

Whales are identified by their flukes.

Reference: (http://www.alaskahumpbacks.org/matching.html)

572.

Sloths don't fart.

Reference: (https://www.bbc.co.uk/bbcthree/article/47750bfb-68c4-4eb1-9676-911ec5945f8b)

573.

Flamingos are not born pink.

Reference: (https://www.youtube.com/watch?v=zhVPoll3LUA)

574.

Corporations would pay to put on a full, professional, Broadway musical as a motivator and reward for their staff.

Reference: (https://en.wikipedia.org/wiki/Industrial_musical)

575.

Maurice Tillet, "The French Angel", was a professional wrestler that suffered from acromegaly, an abnormality of the pituitary gland that causes wild and increased bone growth. While it's not official, it's speculated that Shrek's appearance was based off of his.

Reference: (https://odditiesbizarre.com/maurice-tillet-the-french-angel/)

576.

The first reported death attributed to a video game happened in 1982 when Peter Burkowski, an 18-year-old, had a heart attack playing "Berzerk."

Reference: (http://home.hiwaay.net/~lkseitz/cvg/death.html)

577.

Female kangaroos have 3 vaginas.

Reference: (https://grist.org/animals/kangaroo-genitals-are-weirder-than-you-ever-thought-possible-2/)

578.

The Migrant Mother featured in Dorothea Lange's iconic Dirty Thirties photograph was born Florence Leona Christie, a Cherokee, in a teepee in Indian Territory, Oklahoma, in 1903.

Reference:
(http://www.pbs.org/wgbh/roadshow/stories/articles/2014/4/14/migrant-mother-dorothea-lange/)

579.

Alan Dershowitz is a nudist.

Reference: (http://www.mvmagazine.com/news/2008/08/01/going-au-naturel)

580.

The Zimbabwean dollar had an inflation of 500.000.000.000% per day in mid-November, 2008, and it lost 99% of its value every 8 hours and 42 minutes.

Reference: (https://en.wikipedia.org/wiki/Zimbabwean_dollar)

581.

The first T.V commercial ever was aired in July, 1941, and the name of the company was Bulova watches.

Reference: (https://youtu.be/gZ-dkUjh9SA)

582.

The word "broadcast" was originally used to describe the spreading, or casting, of seeds by hand. It wasn't until 1921 that it was used to describe radio transmission.

Reference: (https://www.dailywritingtips.com/broadcast-vs-broadcasted-as-past-form/)

583.

Over 20 Iraqis were killed by stray celebratory gunfire rounds celebrating the deaths of Uday and Qusay Hussein.

Reference: (https://en.wikipedia.org/wiki/Celebratory_gunfire#Middle_East)

584.

Gretna Green, Scotland, not Las Vegas, is historically the elopement capital of the world, the choice for runaway-wedding couples as far back as 1754.

Reference: (https://en.wikipedia.org/wiki/Gretna_Green)

585.

In 1844, the Whig Party's nominee for U.S. President, Henry Clay, used the official campaign slogan: "Who is James K. Polk?".

Reference: (https://www.presidentsusa.net/campaignslogans.html)

586.

Detonators are strapped to the top of rails by railroad repair crews near their work area. When a stray train runs over the detonator, it sets off the charge, alerting them and getting the driver's attention. They are still used in the U.K. and Australia.

Reference: (https://en.wikipedia.org/wiki/Detonator_(railway))

587.

Antimony pills were used as a purgative and laxative which would pass intact through the gastrointestinal tract. This allowed it to be used over and over again as it is passed down through the generations, so long as you fish it out from the fecal matter.

Reference: (https://en.wikipedia.org/wiki/Antimony_pill)

588.

95% of all copper ever mined was extracted after 1900. More than half has been extracted in the last 24 years.

Reference: (https://en.wikipedia.org/wiki/Copper#Reserves)

589.

VHEMT, Voluntary Human Extinction Movement, is an environmental movement that calls for all people to not reproduce. They support human extinction primarily to prevent environmental degradation.

Reference:
(https://en.wikipedia.org/wiki/Voluntary_Human_Extinction_Movement)

590.

The most successful hunter among apex predators is the African wild dog, with greater than 60% of their chases ending in a kill, which is much higher than that of a lion and hyena.

Reference:
(https://en.wikipedia.org/wiki/African_wild_dog#Hunting_and_feeding_behaviours)

591.

Canada recognizes England's Queen Elisabeth II as the monarch of Canada.

Reference: (http://mentalfloss.com/article/53036/10-things-queen-england-still-does-canada)

592.

After the U.S. took over the Philippines they forced the country to adopt the Fourth of July as their new "Independence Day." U.S. armed forces even delayed declaring victory in the American-Philippines war until July 4th to have a two part victory and Independence Day parade.

Reference: (https://www.theatlantic.com/international/archive/2012/07/the-one-other-country-that-celebrates-the-fourth-of-july-sort-of/259410/)

593.

Cass Elliott and Keith Moon died in the same London Flat, in the same room, 4 years apart, both aged 32.

Reference: (https://en.wikipedia.org/wiki/Cass_Elliot)

594.

Thomas Jefferson created his own version of the Bible, using a razor to cut out the "supernatural" parts, such as the miracles and the resurrection. Today, new members of Congress receive a copy upon election.

Reference: (https://en.wikipedia.org/wiki/Jefferson_Bible)

595.

The striped hyena is extremely trainable and easily tamed. With proper training they can become affectionate and as amenable as well trained dogs.

Reference:
(https://en.wikipedia.org/wiki/Striped_hyena#Tameability)

596.

Tsar Bomba was the single most physically powerful device ever deployed by mankind. Tested in 1961, the Tsar had an explosive power equivalent to about 1,570 times the combined energy of the bombs that destroyed Hiroshima and Nagasaki.

Reference: (https://en.wikipedia.org/wiki/Tsar_Bomba)

597.

Virginia Hall was one of the most highly decorated spies in American history. Her small resistance team is credited with destroying four bridges, derailing dozens of freight trains, killing 150 German soldiers, and capturing another 300 enemy troops. She did all of this with a wooden leg.

Reference:
(http://www.badassoftheweek.com/index.cgi?id=7164420669)

598.

The planet Uranus was originally named "George" after the British King George III.

Reference: (https://en.wikipedia.org/wiki/Uranus)

599.

Although Michael Jackson voiced the character Leon Kompowsky on the Simpson's episode "Stark Raving Dad," he brought in a sound alike to sing "Happy Birthday Lisa."

Reference: (https://youtu.be/DtJ28qOEG1g?t=52m11s)

600.

There was a legislative initiative to add more justices to the U.S. Supreme Court to obtain favorable rulings on New Deal legislation that the Supreme Court had ruled unconstitutional. Preventing this "court packing plan" included the famous "Switch in time that saved nine."

Reference:
(https://en.wikipedia.org/wiki/Judicial_Procedures_Reform_Bill_of_1937)

601.

The referee of a football match can give himself a red card.

Reference: (https://www.independent.ie/sport/soccer/referee-gives-himself-red-card-25998268.html)

602.

Emma Kitchener, wife of Julian Fellowes, creator of Downton Abbey, is descended from Field Marshal Horatio Kitchener, the face of Britain's "Your Country Needs You" recruitment poster.

Reference:
(https://www.telegraph.co.uk/news/picturegalleries/celebritynews/8757793/Julian-Fellowes-inheritance-laws-denying-my-wife-a-title-are-outrageous.html)

603.

Before the fruit, the color orange had no name, it was basically known as a "yellow-red". The earliest known usage of the word "orange" to refer to the fruit is around the 13th century. The earliest use of the word "orange" to refer to the color is the 16th century.

Reference: (https://www.independent.co.uk/news/science/which-came-first-orange-the-colour-or-orange-the-fruit-a6879541.html?amp)

604.

In 2017, the band Phish played thirteen concerts in a row at Madison Square Garden, and performed 237 songs without repeating a single one.

Reference: (https://www.jambase.com/article/number-line-phish-bakers-dozen-residency-numbers)

605.

New York City was briefly renamed "New Orange" after the Dutch regained control of the colony in 1673.

Reference:
(https://en.wikipedia.org/wiki/History_of_New_York_City)

606.

Due to a duodenal ulcer that kept him bedridden for several days, Mussolini lived on a diet of milk and crackers for over a year. Newspapers were forbidden to print anything about his odd diet since the dictator believed it would ruin his macho image.

Reference: (https://theamericanmag.com/il-duces-crackers/)

607.

Third degree burns aren't the most severe category. The most severe burns are 6th degree burns, which have penetrated skin and started to char bone.

Reference: (https://www.walkermorgan.com/fourth-fifth-sixth-degrees/)

608.

Alan Turing was charged with "gross indecency" after self-reporting a burglary and telling the police about the relationship he had with a man he suspected was involved. He chose chemical castration as his sentence. This caused him to grow breasts, become depressed, which were triggers for his suicide.

Reference: (https://paidpost.nytimes.com/the-weinstein-company/world-war-iis-greatest-hero-the-true-story-of-alan-turing.html)

609.

There is a Greek wedding tradition where brides write the names of their single girlfriends on the bottom of their wedding day shoes, and the first woman's name to be erased will be the next to get married.

Reference: (https://www.greekboston.com/wedding/bridal-shoes-tradition/)

610.

A sailor charged with murder committed suicide in the brig at Camp Pendleton by asphyxiating himself by stuffing toilet paper in his mouth.

Reference: (http://www.nydailynews.com/news/world/sailor-charged-murder-commits-suicide-choking-toilet-paper-article-1.396497)

611.

Dora the Explorer teaches English in all languages, except of course, in English, where she teaches Spanish.

Reference: (https://www.verywellfamily.com/fun-facts-about-dora-the-explorer-2765068)

612.

In 2001, former U.S. army reserve officer Jonathan Idema secretly invaded Afghanistan, planning to identify and capture terrorists. For years, he ran a secret private prison and tortured Afghan citizens suspected of terrorism. It is likely that most of his victims were actually innocent.

Reference: (https://en.wikipedia.org/wiki/Jonathan_Idema)

613.

The first print of Led Zeppelin II had such a high dynamic range that on cheap equipment the needle literally jumped out of the groove, and after the daughter of the studio executive complained about the issue, the studio went on to "fix" it with inferior album printing.

Reference: (https://www.wired.com/2015/03/hot-stampers/)

614.

In 2010, a man from the West Midlands, U.K., was arrested for recording his neighbor's noisy dogs and playing the noise back at his neighbor.

Reference:
(https://www.telegraph.co.uk/news/uknews/7966229/Neighbour-records-barking-dog-and-plays-it-back-at-full-volume.html)

615.

The "God of the gaps" is a term used to describe observations of theological perspectives in which gaps in scientific knowledge are taken to be evidence or proof of God's existence.

Reference: (https://en.wikipedia.org/wiki/God_of_the_gaps)

616.

A study found that injecting healthy men with testosterone will significantly increase their lean mass even if they don't exercise at all. While men who also did strength training had the best gains, the testosterone users who didn't exercise also gained more mass than the non-users who did.

Reference:
(https://www.nejm.org/doi/full/10.1056/NEJM199607043350101)

617.

Blue fireworks are the Holy Grail of the pyrotechnic world because the chemistry needs to be absolutely perfect to produce them.

Reference:
(https://www.npr.org/templates/story/story.php?storyId=198781855)

618.

The Intermediate Value Theorem implies that there are always two points on opposite ends of the Earth that have the same temperature and atmospheric pressure.

Reference:
(https://en.wikipedia.org/wiki/Intermediate_value_theorem)

619.

The character of Brain, from "Pinky and the Brain," was based off of Orson Welles, and was directly inspired by tape of Welles being cranky during the taping of a commercial.

Reference: (https://www.adweek.com/creativity/not-so-finest-hours-orson-welles-16175/)

620.

Ian Hart, the actor who played Professor Quirrell in "Harry Potter and the Sorcerer's Stone" had to return to stage acting, which he hates, and once lunged at an audience member for talking during a performance.

Reference: (https://www.theguardian.com/stage/2009/nov/25/ian-hart-lunges-at-audience-member)

621.

The first ever "TreeHuggers" were in 1730s India, hugging trees to defy a King that wanted to build a Grand Palace.

Reference: (https://nvdatabase.swarthmore.edu/content/bishnoi-villagers-sacrifice-lives-save-trees-1730)

622.

The 1978 album "D.o.A: The Third & Final Report of Throbbing Gristle" had false track markers to make it appear that there were 16 tracks of exactly equal length. Its single "United", gaining popularity, was included but sped up to reduce its length from over 4 minutes to just 16 seconds.

Reference:(https://en.wikipedia.org/wiki/D.o.A:_The_Third_and_Final_Report_of_Throbbing_Gristle)

623.

Kate Capshaws' opening scene dress in "Indiana Jones and the Temple of Doom" was one of a kind, made from original 1920s beads. Before the scene was shot, an elephant was able to partially eat it requiring emergency repair work.

Reference:
(https://en.wikipedia.org/wiki/Indiana_Jones_and_the_Temple_of_Doom#Filming)

624.

The 1972 film "Deliverance" brought a surge of whitewater rafting tourists to Rabun County, Georgia, where the movie was filmed. It is now a $20 million per year industry in the region.

Reference:
(https://en.wikipedia.org/wiki/Deliverance#Influence_of_the_film)

625.

A tree in Scotland has "eaten" many metal objects, including a bicycle and, reputedly, a ship's anchor and chain.

Reference: (https://en.wikipedia.org/wiki/Bicycle_Tree_(Trossachs))

626.

Summer blockbusters got their start when James Carrier installed an air cooling system in Paramount's Rivoli Theater in Times Square during a 1925 heat wave.

Reference:(http://www.slate.com/articles/arts/culturebox/2011/07/a_history_of_air_conditioning.html)

627.

In 1903, part of President William McKinley's defense for the annexation of the Philippines was, "there was nothing left for us to do but to take them all, and to educate the Filipinos, and uplift and civilize and Christianize them."

Reference:
(http://historymatters.gmu.edu/blackboard/mckinley.html)

628.

A number 2 hit in the U.K., "O Superman" was over 8 minutes long, and consisted largely of just the word "ha" repeated over and over, with a few synthesized lyrics over the top.

Reference: (https://en.wikipedia.org/wiki/O_Superman)

629.

In 2005, the word "mate" was banned in the Australian Federal Parliament. The ban was revoked within 24 hours.

Reference: (http://www.abc.net.au/news/2005-10-31/parliament-mate-ban-an-error-of-judgment/2135520)

630.

There is a berry when consumed will change your taste buds. It will make vinegar taste like apple juice and lemon and Tabasco taste like candy.

Reference:
(https://www.nytimes.com/2008/05/28/dining/28flavor.html)

631.

When Märket was considered no man's land, the lighthouse was placed on the highest point of the island. However, this meant it was in the Swedish part of the island. Because of this, the border was readjusted in 1985 so that the lighthouse would be in Finland.

Reference: (https://en.wikipedia.org/wiki/M%C3%A4rket)

632.

The United Nation's intervention in 1992, during the Somali Civil War, to deliver humanitarian aid, is estimated to have saved up to 100,000 lives.

Reference: (https://en.wikipedia.org/wiki/Unified_Task_Force)

633.

The Air Mobility Command's 89th Airlift Wing of the U.S. Air Force currently maintains two identical Air Force 1 Boeing 747-200B planes at Joint Base Andrews, Maryland for presidential use: SAM 28000 and SAM 29000. One is always ready, even when the other is in maintenance.

Reference: (https://www.cbsnews.com/pictures/a-tour-of-air-force-one/4/)

634.

There's a black market for sand.

Reference: (https://www.wired.com/2015/03/illegal-sand-mining/)

635.

After the Crusaders captured Jerusalem, they massacred the Jew and Muslim population, including women and children. The massacre was so large, that the Crusaders were supposedly wading in blood up to their ankles.

Reference:
(https://en.wikipedia.org/wiki/Siege_of_Jerusalem_(1099)#Massacre
)

636.

A bear does not actually hibernate, instead it just slows down by going into a deep sleep for up to 100 days.

Reference: (http://www.bigcat.org/news/the-truth-about-bears-and-hibernation)

637.

The most common road name in England and Wales is High Street, but in Scotland its Main Street, while the second most common in England is Church Lane, but in Scotland and Wales it's Station Road.

Reference: (https://www.family-tree.co.uk/news-and-views/news/the-30-most-common-street-names-in-england-scotland-and-wales-what-do)

638.

Before Ralph Fiennes was cast as Lord Voldemort, Rowan Atkinson was originally rumored to have gotten the role.

Reference:
(http://news.bbc.co.uk/cbbcnews/hi/world/newsid_3376000/3376933.stm)

639.

Camels do not store water in their humps. The humps are actually reservoirs for fatty tissue. Concentrating fat in their humps minimizes insulation throughout the rest of the body, thus allowing camels to survive in such extreme hot regions.

Reference: (https://onekindplanet.org/animal/camel/)

640.

The largest purchase ever made on the AMEX Centurion Card was a $170 million painting.

Reference: (http://www.businessinsider.com/how-to-fly-free-forever-put-170-million-on-your-amex-2015-11)

641.

A poll by Planet Rock Radio in 2005 asked around 3,500 listeners to create their fantasy super group by picking their favorite star for each respective instrument. They ended up choosing all the members of Led Zeppelin.

Reference: (http://news.bbc.co.uk/2/hi/entertainment/4669597.stm)

642.

A woman claimed that Concorde's sonic booms made her pregnant because it interrupted her rhythm method of contraception.

Reference:
(https://www.youtube.com/watch?v=MVcig2pi9qs&feature=youtu.be&t=1270)

643.

John Capes was the man who swam from sunken submarine at 170 feet and survived. A world record so impossible people thought him a liar until after his death.

Reference: (https://owlcation.com/humanities/World-War-2-History-John-Capes-Amazing-Submarine-Escape)

644.

When Michael Jackson's car broke down once in Beverly Hills, he called 911 for help. He was advised to only use 911 in emergency situations. He was very surprised when they refused to assist him, even after he told them that he was Michael Jackson.

Reference: (https://consequenceofsound.net/2017/04/the-unsolved-controversies-of-michael-jackson/)

645.

Kanye West samples Counter Strike: Global Offensive on his hit song "Ultralight Beam".

Reference: (https://genius.com/a/this-hidden-counter-strike-sample-on-kanye-west-s-ultralight-beam-will-blow-your-mind)

646.

The first integrated circuits were made in the 1920's by Loewe and included up to three triodes, tetrodes or pentodes and several passive elements in the same vacuum tube enclosure. These devices implemented almost an entire radio receiver in that one enclosure.

Reference: (http://electricstuff.co.uk/loewe.html)

647.

A catcher once performed a "hidden ball trick" by literally throwing a potato into the left field.

Reference: (http://articles.latimes.com/2012/feb/23/sports/la-sp-sn-sports-urban-legend-potato-20120223)

648.

The Oscar award for best foreign film is given to the country, not the director.

Reference: (https://www.vox.com/cards/oscars-2017-nominations-categories/oscars-foreign-film)

649.

In 1936, Congress considered adding Susan B. Anthony to Mount Rushmore. Even Eleanor Roosevelt wrote a letter to the sculptor requesting it.

Reference: (https://www.npca.org/articles/1755-a-woman-on-mount-rushmore)

650.

Dogs can smell cancer with relatively high accuracy.

Reference: (http://www.aaha.org/blog/NewStat/post/2017/03/28/364954/Dogs-sniff-out-breast-cancer.aspx)

651.

Poisonous beauty advice for Victorian women included: Lead face paint; Mercury for eye treatments; Belladonna drops from the deadly nightshade plant used for the "dilated pupil is cool" look. Bathing in arsenic springs was highly recommended.

Reference: (https://www.atlasobscura.com/articles/the-poisonous-beauty-advice-columns-of-victorian-england)

652.

Although considered one of the most toxic animals on Earth, if a poison dart frogs is raised in captivity, it will never develop venom. This is likely because they assimilate plant poisons which are carried by their prey.

Reference:
(https://www.nationalgeographic.com/animals/amphibians/g/golden-poison-frog/)

653.

The ostrich has the largest eye of any land animal, measuring almost 5 centimeters across, allowing predators such as lions to be seen at long distances.

Reference: (https://onekindplanet.org/animal/ostrich/)

654.

There was a fire at the North Orange Blossom Trail warehouse in 1991. It burned so hot they couldn't put it out with water because it separated the hydrogen and oxygen.

Reference: (http://articles.orlandosentinel.com/1993-11-08/news/9311080226_1_chevron-hta-asbestos)

655.

Whales are struck by large ships, and can get caught on the "bulbous bow" under the waterline.

Reference: (http://www.professionalmariner.com/October-November-2013/whale-zones/)

656.

"Natsubate" is a Japanese word for the lethargy that comes with hot summer weather.

Reference:
(https://www.japantimes.co.jp/life/2007/07/17/lifestyle/how-to-survive-summer-fatigue/#.WzrfzdJKhPY)

657.

Geertruida Wijsmuller-Meijer was a Dutch woman who saved 10,000 Jewish children by charming and bribing Dutch train workers and German officers including a young Adolf Eichmann. Research suggests she saved more Jewish lives than all but Raoul Wallenberg.

Reference: (https://wikipedia.org/wiki/Geertruida_Wijsmuller-Meijer)

658.

Prudence Crandall was a school teacher in Connecticut who made history in 1832 when she accepted an African American girl, Sarah Harris, into her class, making it the first integrated school house in the U.S.

Reference: (https://en.wikipedia.org/wiki/Prudence_Crandall)

659.

The Ancient Egyptians were the first to follow a calendar consisting 365 days, including 12 months of 30 days and 5 extra days at the end.

Reference: (https://www.britannica.com/science/Egyptian-calendar)

660.

In 1963, a Russian "Sully" had to ditch a twin engine airliner in the Volga River, and everyone survived.

Reference: (https://www.youtube.com/watch?v=P3hbsYDpeto)

661.

Blues singer "Screamin' Jay Hawkins" was fed up with song about love or heartbreak back in the 1960's, so he wrote a song about constipation.

Reference: (https://www.youtube.com/watch?v=ic3g8Xnf7LI)

662.

The inventor of the trapeze also invented the leotard. His name was Jules Leotard.

Reference: (http://www.vam.ac.uk/content/articles/j/jules-leotard/)

663.

Dolphins sleep by resting one side of the brain at a time. This allows them to continue rising to the surface for air and to keep an eye open to watch out for predators.

Reference: (https://onekindplanet.org/animal/dolphin/)

664.

The Western Lowlands Gorillas scientific name is "Gorilla gorilla gorilla."

Reference: (https://seaworld.org/en/animal-info/animal-infobooks/gorilla/scientific-classification)

665.

In 2001, Chicago Bears safety Mike Brown scored back-to-back overtime game-winning touchdowns off interceptions. This is the only time a team has scored two touchdowns of any time in back-to-back overtime games.

Reference:
(https://www.youtube.com/watch?v=MRp3fDKHYJo&t=2m0s)

666.

In Washington D.C., building height is limited to be the lesser of 130 feet or the width of the street in front.

Reference:
(https://en.wikipedia.org/wiki/Height_of_Buildings_Act_of_1910)

667.

The Terminator's world-famous phrase "Hasta la vista, baby" is translated to "Sayonara, baby" in the Spanish version of the film, to preserve the humorous nature.

Reference: (https://www.youtube.com/watch?v=L3pzZXOixKc)

668.

There are 43 buildings in New York City assigned to their own exclusive ZIP code. The original World Trade Center complex had its own, 10048, but the new complex shares a ZIP code with the surrounding area.

Reference: (https://untappedcities.com/2013/08/16/cities-101-buildings-with-exclusive-zip-codes-nyc/)

669.

The U.S. Treasury has a mutilated currency division and offers a free service of replacing damaged dollar bills.

Reference: (https://bep.gov/services/currencyredemption.html)

670.

The lead singer of Toto was the singing voice for adult Simba in The Lion King.

Reference:
(https://en.wikipedia.org/wiki/Joseph_Williams_(musician))

671.

Legendary guitarist Django Reinhardt received first and second-degree burns on his left hand when he was 18 and was told he would never be able to play guitar again, but by sheer will he taught himself to play using only his thumb, index and middle finger.

Reference:
(https://en.wikipedia.org/wiki/Django_Reinhardt#Marriage_and_inju
ry)

672.

In 1936, Orson Welles directed an entirely African American cast in a production of Macbeth set in the Caribbean, nicknamed "Voodoo Macbeth," where Haitian voodoo took the place of Scottish witchcraft.

Reference: (https://www.youtube.com/watch?v=QZLrqJka-EU)

673.

The most common street name in the United States is Second Street.

Reference: (https://www.nlc.org/most-common-us-street-names)

674.

On February 7, 1812, a series of earthquakes near Missouri were so strong that they caused the Mississippi River to flow backwards for several hours.

Reference: (https://www.history.com/this-day-in-history/earthquake-causes-fluvial-tsunami-in-mississippi)

675.

The first 3 Space Shuttle landings were on dried lake beds, not concrete runways.

Reference: (https://en.wikipedia.org/wiki/STS-3)

676.

Ayahuasca had been patented by a U.S. business man and he held the patent for over a decade.

Reference: (http://www.singingtotheplants.com/2008/01/ayahuasca-patent-case/)

677.

Mary Fields, also known as "Stagecoach Mary," ran a U.S. mail route in Montana for 8 years starting in 1895, protecting the mail from both weather and bandits.

Reference: (https://www.history.com/news/meet-stagecoach-mary-the-daring-black-pioneer-who-protected-wild-west-stagecoaches)

678.

During the Battle of Midway, Austin Merrill flew to attack a Japanese carrier force. Along the way, he lost his bomb due to a malfunction of his dive bomber. Despite this, he dove on the fleet in order to draw anti-aircraft fire away from his squadron. He received the Navy Cross for this action.

Reference:
(http://dogtagexperience.org/mobile/relatedItem.php?id=341)

679.

Zip codes in the U.S. increase in an east-to-west fashion.

Reference:
(https://en.wikipedia.org/wiki/ZIP_Code#Structure_and_allocation)

680.

In 1989, a naked man climbed a flagpole at a McDonald's in Anchorage, Alaska. He stretched his arms out and nosedived onto the pavement. There were no drugs in his system, and he has never been identified.

Reference: (https://www.anchoragepress.com/news/unearthing-the-truth/article_af2602b1-c7fe-595d-8d8e-bd6a2359d0de.html)

681.

A French astronomer named Guillaume Le Gentil spent 8 years of his life on a quest to observe the transit of Venus, during which he was declared legally dead and his wife remarried, only for the sky to end up being cloudy on the day of the transit.

Reference: (https://en.wikipedia.org/wiki/Guillaume_Le_Gentil)

682.

Naked mole-rats don't appear to age. Unlike other mammals, they show no physiological decline and their mortality rate doesn't increase as they grow older.

Reference: (https://elifesciences.org/articles/31157)

683.

10 Nazi concentration camps had brothels of female prisoners for prisoners as incentive to work hard and boost morale. It was a failure as few men were physically able for sex, nor could they afford the 15 minutes, missionary only appointment that was often supervised via peep hole.

Reference: (https://www.reuters.com/article/us-germany-nazis-brothels/new-book-reveals-horror-of-nazi-camp-brothels-idUSTRE57G45X20090817)

684.

A New Zealand man changed his name to "Full Metal Havok More Sexy N Intelligent Than Spock And All The Superheroes Combined With Frostnova" after losing a drunken bet at a poker game.

Reference:
(https://www.telegraph.co.uk/news/newstopics/howaboutthat/10687002/New-Zealand-man-given-ridiculous-99-character-name-after-losing-poker-bet.html)

685.

Baywatch lasted only one season on NBC before being cancelled. After syndication rights were acquired, it lasted another 8 seasons not including spin-offs and films.

Reference: (https://en.wikipedia.org/wiki/Baywatch)

686.

You explicitly cannot bring catapults to the Temple of Heaven in Beijing.

Reference:
(http://en.tiantanpark.com/ShowContent2.aspx?Sortid=11)

687.

Zambia is the only country to have entered the Olympics as one country, Northern Rhodesia, and left the games as another. Zambia declared independence on the last day of the 1964 Tokyo Olympics.

Reference: (https://en.wikipedia.org/wiki/Zambia#Sports)

688.

The song "Operator" by Jim Croce was inspired during Jim Croce's military service, where he saw lines of soldiers waiting to use the outdoor phone on base, many of them calling their wives or girlfriends to see if their Dear John letter was true.

Reference:
(https://en.wikipedia.org/wiki/Operator_(That%27s_Not_the_Way_I t_Feels))

689.

In 2009, Gibson was poised to release a line of low-end Hendrix-inspired Stratocasters. The backlash was so harsh for being such a poor representation of Jimi's legacy that they were never released to the public.

Reference: (http://www.myrareguitars.com/gibson-creates-signature-jimi-hendrix-strat)

690.

Continents drift at about the same speed as fingernails grow.

Reference:
(https://www.nytimes.com/2016/07/23/science/continental-drift-tectonic-plates.html)

691.

Whanganui River is legally recognized as a person in New Zealand.

Reference: (https://en.wikipedia.org/wiki/Whanganui_River)

692.

Countless would-be adventurers have been rescued attempting to reach the bus where Chris McCandless died in "Into the Wild," as well as three known instances of fans being found dead.

Reference: (http://blogrope.com/travel/9-interesting-facts-you-should-know-about-the-movie-into-the-wild/)

693.

The Utah Jazz are still paying their draft pick from 1993; $153,000 per year even though he only played for one season.

Reference: (https://www.nytimes.com/1996/04/04/sports/sports-people-basketball-wright-leaves-psychiatric-hospital.html)

694.

A former Crown Prince of Thailand, Maha Vajiralongkorn, had a poodle called Fufu. The poodle was not only an Air Chief Marshal, but followed him on royal engagements.

Reference: (https://en.wikipedia.org/wiki/Fufu_(dog))

695.

There is a parasite that attaches to a fishes tongue and severs the blood vessels causing the tongue to fall off. It then attaches itself to the stub of what was once its tongue and becomes the fish's new tongue.

Reference: (https://en.wikipedia.org/wiki/Cymothoa_exigua)

696.

The "Inception Hotel" scenes were actually filmed in a giant centrifuge.

Reference: (https://youtu.be/8PhiSSnaUKk)

697.

Isokelekel was a folk hero of Pohnpei who committed suicide by tying his penis to the top of a bent young palm tree, then releasing the tree, ripping off his penis and bleeding to death.

Reference: (https://mrpsmythopedia.wikispaces.com/Isokelekel)

698.

In the Batman Treaty, Melbourne, Australia, was purchased from the Native's for various items including 4 flannel jackets, 150 pounds of flour, and 62 pairs of scissors.

Reference: (https://en.wikipedia.org/wiki/Batman%27s_Treaty)

699.

After the 9/11 attacks, the stock exchanges did not open on September 11 and remained closed until September 17. The U.S. stocks lost $1.4 trillion in value for the week.

Reference: (https://en.wikipedia.org/wiki/September_11_attacks.)

700.

In the oldest preserved manuscript of Revelations the number of the beast is 616, not 666.

Reference: (https://en.wikipedia.org/wiki/Number_of_the_Beast)

701.

Water striders are predatory, feeding on other live insects that fall into the water by liquefying and slowly sucking out their innards.

Reference: (https://youtu.be/E2unnSK7WTE)

702.

A man named David Hahn tried to make a homemade nuclear breeder reactor in his backyard shed. Though the reactor never reached critical mass, it irradiated his backyard and his mother's property would be a Superfund cleanup site for 10 months.

Reference: (https://en.wikipedia.org/wiki/David_Hahn)

703.

The first successful bridge to be made of iron opened to traffic in 1781 in Shropshire, England. The locals were so proud of their new bridge that they renamed the town on the other side Ironbridge.

Reference: (https://en.wikipedia.org/wiki/The_Iron_Bridge)

704.

There is a term for the tendency of technical equipment to fail when certain people are present. It's called the Pauli effect, named after Wolfgang Ernst Pauli.

Reference: (https://en.wikipedia.org/wiki/Pauli_effect)

705.

Ulysses S. Grant not only created the Department of Justice, he also supported the Fifteenth Amendment and asked Congress to pass the Civil Rights Act of 1871, allowing him to combat and prosecute the Ku Klux Klan.

Reference:
(https://en.wikipedia.org/wiki/Presidency_of_Ulysses_S._Grant)

706.

The commonly-held belief that the children's song "Ring Around the Rosy" is actually about the Black Plague is an urban legend from the 1950's. The song's lyrics likely have nothing to do with death or disease.

Reference:
(https://en.wikipedia.org/wiki/Ring_a_Ring_o%27_Roses)

707.

Italy had attack boats designed to climb up-and-over obstacles in World War I.

Reference: (http://www.naval-encyclopedia.com/ww1/Italy/grillo-class-tracked-torpedo-launches/)

708.

Ignosticism or igtheism is the idea that the question of the existence of God is meaningless because the term "god" has no coherent and unambiguous definition and that every other theological position assumes too much about the concept of god and many other theological concepts.

Reference: (https://en.wikipedia.org/wiki/Ignosticism)

709.

Sarah McLachlan was once sued by an obsessed fan because she used one of his delusional letters as the basis for her hit song "Possession." He committed suicide before it went to court.

Reference: (https://www.rollingstone.com/music/music-news/interview-sarah-mclachlan-86779/)

710.

The Guinness Book of World Records has vehemently refused to validate any attempt at the world record for the longest time spent awake, believing that it's dangerous to human health. The current record is 264 hours or around 11 days, which was set by a high school student as a science project.

Reference: (http://www.bbc.com/future/story/20180118-the-boy-who-stayed-awake-for-11-days)

711.

In 1991, the New Kids on the Block topped the Forbes list of highest paid entertainers, beating out the likes of Michael Jackson, Madonna, Prince, and Bill Cosby.

Reference: (https://en.wikipedia.org/wiki/New_Kids_on_the_Block)

712.

Beetles are the most diverse order of life on our planet and have been around since the days of Pangaea.

Reference: (https://lovenature.vhx.tv/macro-worlds/videos/macroworlds-103-gods-darlings-beetles)

713.

The Dire Straits were inducted into the Rock and Roll Hall of Fame in 2018. Lead man Mark Knopfler was ranked 27th on Rolling Stone's list of greatest guitarists of all time. There is an asteroid and a dinosaur species named after him.

Reference:
(https://en.wikipedia.org/wiki/Mark_Knopfler#Personal_life)

714.

Halle Berry's stunt double in "Catwoman" was a man. Hawaiian-born Nito Larioza was the same height and skin color and wore red lipstick and a cat suit for the filming.

Reference: (http://cinema.com/news/item/7091/halles-stunt-double-is-a-man.phtml)

715.

The word "mesmerized" refers to the work of Franz Friedrich Anton Mesmer. He also introduced the term, "animal magnetism" and is credited with discovering hypnosis.

Reference: (https://www.ncbi.nlm.nih.gov/pubmed/20166775)

716.

The former U.S. soccer star Brian McBride credits headbanging to Metallica, AC/DC and Judas Priest for being able to generate so much power on headers. He scored the lone U.S. goal in the 1998 FIFA World Cup with his head.

Reference: (https://www.wnycstudios.org/story/american-fiasco-roger-bennett-world-cup-ends)

717.

A serial arsonist in California worked as an arson investigator and fire captain, and would commit arson on his way to and from arson investigator conferences. Before his arrest, he even wrote a novel about a firefighter who was a serial arsonist.

Reference: (https://en.wikipedia.org/wiki/John_Leonard_Orr)

718.

The word "denim" is derived from the French words "de Nîmes", translating to "from Nîmes."

Reference:
(https://en.wikipedia.org/wiki/Denim#Etymology_and_origin)

719.

The Rhind Mathematical Papyrus, written 1000 years before Pythogoras, shows how to find the volume of cylindrical and rectangular granaries as well as how to find the area of a circle.

Reference: (https://owlcation.com/stem/What-is-Trigonometry)

720.

On September 8th, 1935, in Baton Rouge, Louisiana, senator Huey Long was assassinated by Carl Weiss. Years later, the case was reopened, and it was revealed that senator Long was accidentally shot to death by his bodyguards, who opened fire on Carl Weiss when he pulled out his gun.

Reference: (http://unsolvedmysteries.wikia.com/wiki/Huey_Long)

721.

The word "quarantine" comes from the 40-day period, or "quaranti giorni," that ships were required to wait outside of the port Venice, Italy during the time of the Black Death.

Reference: (https://history.howstuffworks.com/historical-events/black-death2.htm)

722.

Shakespeare accidentally burnt down his theatre once.

Reference: (https://www.telegraph.co.uk/only-in-britain/fire-destroy-globe-theatre/)

723.

Viewing a stressful soccer match more than doubles the risk of an acute cardiovascular event.

Reference: (https://www.nejm.org/doi/full/10.1056/nejmoa0707427)

724.

Methamphetamine can be prescribed to children under the name Desoxyn for the treatment of ADHD.

Reference: (https://www.mayoclinic.org/drugs-supplements/methamphetamine-oral-route/description/drg-20071824)

725.

Lidocaine is often added to cocaine as a diluent, this is why it numbs the gums when applied. This often gives users the impression of high quality cocaine, when in actuality the user is receiving a diluted product.

Reference: (https://en.wikipedia.org/wiki/Lidocaine#Adulterant_in_cocaine)

726.

There existed a tree swastika in a German forest that went unnoticed for nearly 60 years.

Reference: (https://en.wikipedia.org/wiki/Forest_swastika)

727.

A village named Monowi in Nebraska has only one resident, Elsie Eiler.

Reference: (https://en.wikipedia.org/wiki/Monowi,_Nebraska)

728.

The official divorce complaint of Mary Louise Bell, wife of world-famous physicist Richard Feynman, was that, "He begins working calculus problems in his head as soon as he awakens. He did calculus while driving in his car, while sitting in the living room, and while lying in bed at night."

Reference:
(https://en.wikipedia.org/wiki/Richard_Feynman#Personal_and_political_life)

729.

In the early days of football, before penalty shoot-outs were a thing, the winner of a game that ended with a draw was decided by a simple coin flip.

Reference: (https://en.wikipedia.org/wiki/Penalty_shoot-out_(association_football)#Alternatives)

730.

"Roses are red/Violets are blue" dates back to 1590 with the lines: "In a fresh fountaine, farre from all men's vew//She bath'd her brest, the boyling heat t'allay;// She bath'd with roses red, and violets blew,// And all the sweetest flowres, that in the forrest grew."

Reference: (https://en.wikipedia.org/wiki/Roses_Are_Red#Origins)

731.

The borough Wedding was called "Red Wedding" for being a center of militant communists who regularly clashed with Nazis during the Weimar Republic.

Reference:
(https://en.wikipedia.org/wiki/Wedding_(Berlin)#History)

732.

Female kangaroos can determine the sex of their offspring. They can even delay gestation when environmental factors are likely to diminish the chance of young surviving.

Reference: (https://onekindplanet.org/animal/kangaroo/)

733.

Duke, the Great Pyrenees, has been elected not once, not twice, but three times as mayor of Cormorant, U.S.

Reference: (https://www.huffingtonpost.com/entry/dog-mayor-duke_us_57bbebf5e4b00d9c3a19cb19?m=false)

734.

Warren Buffett won a $1 million dollar bet against a hedge fund. He bet that a simple index fund would outperform a collection of hedge funds over the course of 10 years. He donated the money to charity.

Reference: (http://fortune.com/2017/12/30/warren-buffett-million-dollar-bet/)

735.

Dubai's fake Palm Islands utilize enough sand to fill 2.5 Empire State Buildings.

Reference: (https://www.youtube.com/watch?v=p4DPgJJHhYg)

736.

There is a 1,440,000 square meter enclosed park in Northern China that is filled with about 800 big cats.

Reference: (https://www.nomadasaurus.com/harbin-siberian-tiger-park/)

737.

Sega once released ads for the Sega Dream Gear depicting Game Boy owners as obese and uneducated and even said, "If you were color blind and had an IQ of less than 12, then you wouldn't mind which portable you had."

Reference: (https://en.wikipedia.org/wiki/Game_Gear)

738.

In 2007, a man fell into an active lava flow from the Ol Doinyo Lengai volcano and survived.

Reference:
([https://volcano.si.edu/showreport.cfm?doi=10.5479/si.GVP.BGVN 200802-222120](https://volcano.si.edu/showreport.cfm?doi=10.5479/si.GVP.BGVN200802-222120))

739.

A pig was born with testicles instead of eyes.

Reference: (https://www.perthnow.com.au/lifestyle/bizarre-mutant-pig-with-a-human-face-giant-tongue-and-a-penis-on-its-forehead-is-caught-on-camera-in-china-ng-ac227f36c2cc275adcce659ea3b624b6)

740.

Arwen, from Lord of the Rings, was about 2700 years old when she married Aragorn, who was roughly 90.

Reference: (http://lotr.wikia.com/wiki/Arwen)

741.

Mantis will continue to mate after they have been decapitated, causing them to produce even more sperm.

Reference:
(https://en.wikipedia.org/wiki/Mantis#Sexual_cannibalism)

742.

In the 1950's and 1960's, cheap sandals were called "go-aheads" in California and Hawaii surf culture.

Reference:
(https://www.grammarphobia.com/blog/2013/08/zori.html)

743.

The creator God of Hindu, Brahma has four hands. The first holds the Vedas, knowledge, the second holds Rosary, time, the third holds a Lotus, the means to feed sacrificial fire, and the fourth holds a Water Pot, the means where all creation emanates from.

Reference: (https://en.wikipedia.org/wiki/Brahma)

744.

The Irish government punished Irish citizens who enlisted in the British military during World War II to fight the Nazis.

Reference:
(https://www.telegraph.co.uk/news/uknews/defence/10041215/Ireland-pardons-Second-World-War-soldiers-who-left-to-fight-Nazis.html)

745.

Food in your digestive system is actually considered to be outside of your body.

Reference:
(https://www.merckmanuals.com/home/fundamentals/the-human-body/barriers-on-the-outside-and-the-inside)

746.

Prince's hit song "When Doves Cry" was originally supposed to have a bass line, but he decided that the song would be too conventional with one.

Reference: (https://en.wikipedia.org/wiki/When_Doves_Cry)

747.

Scallions and green onions are the same thing, but chives come from a completely different plant.

Reference: (https://www.huffingtonpost.com/entry/whats-the-difference-between-chives-and-green-onions_us_575af04de4b0ced23ca7e786)

748.

The braille on all drive-thru ATMs is for visually impaired people to use when riding as a rear passenger in a vehicle. Braille on ATMs is federally mandated, and helps maintain financial privacy by allowing blind individuals to bank without having to disclose their pin to a driver.

Reference: (http://www.whsv.com/content/news/476255633.html)

749.

Rihanna was an army cadet in a sub-military program; the singer-songwriter Shontelle was her drill sergeant.

Reference: (https://en.wikipedia.org/wiki/Rihanna)

750.

Chicken parmigiana doesn't have to have parmesan.

Reference: (https://www.montebene.com/blogs/blog-posts/58998467-the-story-behind-the-staple-chicken-parmigiana)

751.

Some World War II Allies that ended up in Switzerland were housed at the Wauwilermoos penal camp. Conditions there were brutal, violating the 1929 Geneva Conventions, and the self-appointed warden was a Nazi sympathizer. The camp was mostly ignored until 2013.

Reference:
(https://en.wikipedia.org/wiki/Wauwilermoos_internment_camp)

752.

The Paralympics aren't just for the physically disabled, but also the intellectually disabled.

Reference: (https://www.bbc.com/news/magazine-19371031)

753.

The five Olympic rings were introduced in 1912 with the five colors representing each and every color that appeared on the flags of the Olympics' competing nations at that time.

Reference: (http://mentalfloss.com/article/31263/what-do-olympic-rings-mean)

754.

Ancient Romans kept phallic wind chimes for good luck and protection against curses.

Reference:
(https://en.wikipedia.org/wiki/Tintinnabulum_(Ancient_Rome))

755.

"Alan Smithee" is an official pseudonym used by film directors who wish to disown a project due to a lack of their creative control.

Reference: (https://en.wikipedia.org/wiki/Alan_Smithee)

756.

In the Lord of the Rings, Gimli was 139 years old when he joined the Fellowship. He also wanted to join his father and Thorin

Oakenshield on their journey to reclaim The Lonely Mountain in The Hobbit, but was denied for being too young at age 62.

Reference: (https://en.wikipedia.org/wiki/Gimli_(Middle-earth))

757.

Shaka, King of the Zulus, would beat the women and children of his soldiers to death if the regiment lost in battle.

Reference: (https://en.wikipedia.org/wiki/Cetshwayo_kaMpande)

758.

The U.S. has had an organization meant to assess the threat of an EMP attack since 2001.

Reference: (http://www.empcommission.org/)

759.

The real life brother of the actress who played "Scout" in "To Kill a Mockingbird" directed "Saturday Night Fever", among others.

Reference:
(https://en.wikipedia.org/wiki/Mary_Badham#Personal_life)

760.

Prior to British troops firing on civilians at the Boston Massacre in 1770, they were pelted with oyster shells, ice, stones, sticks, and beaten with clubs by an unruly mob. At the trial, the soldiers were successfully defended by none other than John Adams and all were acquitted of murder.

Reference: (http://www.famous-trials.com/massacre/196-home)

761.

In 1975, Ingo Bethke escaped from East Germany by floating on an air mattress across the Elbe. 8 years later, his brother Holger fled

East Berlin by firing an arrow with a rope tied to it and zip lining across. The two then flew their brother Egbert over the wall on a homemade ultralight in 1989.

Reference: (http://www.readersdigest.ca/features/heart/escape-east-germany/view-all/)

762.

The actor Charles S. Dutton from "Roc", "Alien 3" and "Rudy" was once imprisoned and sent to solitary confinement, allowed one book and mistakenly grabbed an anthology of black playwrights, liked it so much that he then finished his GED in prison and enrolled in drama school upon his release.

Reference: (https://en.wikipedia.org/wiki/Charles_S._Dutton)

763.

The Mayor of Boston once got the Rolling Stones out of jail.

Reference:
(https://en.wikipedia.org/wiki/Kevin_White_(politician)#Rolling_Stones)

764.

Male tufted deer have sharp canine fangs that can grow as long as an inch, or longer in some rare cases.

Reference: (https://en.wikipedia.org/wiki/Tufted_deer)

765.

The B-24 Liberator is the world's most produced bomber, heavy bomber, multi-engine aircraft, and American military aircraft in history.

Reference: (https://www.britannica.com/technology/B-24)

766.

Angie's List and Home Advisor are the same company.

Reference: (https://techcrunch.com/2017/05/01/angi/)

767.

A French man lied to his family about being a doctor for 18 years, and when about to be found out he murdered his wife, children, parents, and the family dog.

Reference: (https://en.wikipedia.org/wiki/Jean-Claude_Romand)

768.

While serving as a bomber pilot in World War II, Star Trek creator Gene Roddenberry befriended a Chinese pilot called Kim Noonien Singh. Gene tried to reach out to his friend by naming the character Khan Noonien Singh after him, but the attempt failed and the two men never saw each other again.

Reference: (https://www.warhistoryonline.com/instant-articles/creator-star-trek-named-famous-villain-friend-wwii-pilot-days.html)

769.

The coral snake farts as a defense mechanism.

Reference: (http://www.anapsid.org/snakefart.html)

770.

Cherokee Indians had to attend segregated schools because it was assumed Cherokees had African blood.

Reference: (http://www.encyclopediaofarkansas.net/encyclopedia/entry-detail.aspx?entryID=5365)

771.

Heart transplant recipients often report changes in temperament or aesthetic taste which parallel traits of their donor, going as far as pursuing the same hobbies as and adopting the donor's musical tastes.

Reference:
(https://link.springer.com/article/10.1023%2FA%3A1013009425905
)

772.

Radiosynthesis is a process like photosynthesis that uses the pigment melanin to convert gamma radiation into chemical energy for growth. Radiotrophic fungi were discovered in 1991 in and around Chernobyl Nuclear Power Plant.

Reference:
(https://en.wikipedia.org/wiki/Radiosynthesis_(metabolism))

773.

San Francisco International airport does not use the TSA.

Reference: (https://skift.com/2016/05/27/more-airports-may-ditch-the-tsa-and-use-private-security-instead/)

774.

Sir Nicholas Windon saved 669 children, in 1938, from German concentration camps. He kept his heroic deed a secret for 50 years, until his wife found a list of the children's names in their attic.

Reference: (https://youtu.be/WoDW7lDx8uU)

775.

In "Reservoir Dogs," Madonna, who is the main topic of the opening conversation, really liked the film, but refuted Quentin Tarantino's interpretation of her song "Like a Virgin". She gave him a copy of her "Erotica" album, signed, "To Quentin. It's not about dick, it's about love. Madonna."

Reference: (https://wespeakmusic.tv/this-is-how-madonna-responded-after-quentin-tarantino-called-like-a-virgin-a-metaphor-for-big-dicks/)

776.

There are species of tiger moths capable of jamming bat echolocation by producing their own clicks, up to 4500 per second.

Reference:
(https://en.wikipedia.org/wiki/Echolocation_jamming#Jamming_by_prey)

777.

In 1976, the Chicago White Sox uniforms were short pants and big disco collars on the shirts.

Reference: (http://news.sportslogos.net/2016/08/08/a-short-experiment-the-story-of-the-chicago-white-sox-shorts/amp/)

778.

Operation Vulture, the proposed American operation that was seriously considered and which would rescue French forces at the battle of Dien Bien Phu, included the use of nuclear weapons.

Reference: (https://en.wikipedia.org/wiki/Operation_Vulture)

779.

Bees can be blue. Xylocopa caerulea, the blue carpenter bee, is non-aggressive and semi-solitary. They do not build hives like honeybees but instead prefer to live inside dead wood. They live in Southeast Asia, India and Southern China.

Reference: (http://www.australiangeographic.com.au/blogs/creatura-blog/2018/04/the-blue-carpenter-bee)

780.

When A.N. Wilson was writing a biography of the poet John Betjeman, a hoaxer sent Wilson a fake letter purporting to be from Betjeman to his mistress, which Wilson included in the book. He later realized the first letters of each sentence in the letter spelled out "A.N. WILSON IS A SHIT."

Reference:
(https://www.theguardian.com/uk/2006/aug/28/topstories3.books)

781.

Despite having iron, our blood is repelled by magnets instead of being attracted to it.

Reference: (https://www.youtube.com/watch?v=IVsWTkD2M6Q)

782.

In order to control the spider's movements in the 1990 movie "Arachnophobia", filmmakers attached minuscule leashes to their abdomens with wax and in some extreme instances, glued tiny metal plates, controlled by electromagnets, to their stomachs.

Reference: (http://ew.com/article/1990/07/27/wrangling-real-tarantulas-arachnophobia/)

783.

Martin Scorsese has made 27 films in 51 years and none of them had been qualified as a bad movie by critics.

Reference: (http://www.metacritic.com/pictures/film-directors-without-a-single-bad-movie)

784.

Scientists believe that ecstasy is able to help autistic people overcome their social anxiety.

Reference: (http://blogs.discovermagazine.com/d-brief/2017/04/27/ecstasy-autism-therapy/)

785.

Prawns are born as male and, later on, their sex changes to female. In other words, the bigger the prawns are, the more likely they are female.

Reference: (http://www.utas.edu.au/news/2015/8/29/5-sex-change-project-set-to-transform-aquaculture/)

786.

Guillermo del Toro said that he saw a UFO and that "it was horribly designed" and "so clichéd, with lights [blinking]. It's so sad."

Reference: (https://www.hollywoodreporter.com/news/guillermo-del-toro-seeing-a-ufo-hearing-ghosts-shaping-water-1068754)

787.

According to research, big cities tend to be quite liberal. This includes cities in "red states," where voters are often more liberal in practice than in attitude.

Reference:(https://www.oregonlive.com/today/index.ssf/2017/07/buffalo_is_more_progressive_th.html)

788.

Avant-garde film director Alejandro Jodorowsky studied mime under Marcel Marceau, and claims to have invented the "trapped in a glass box" routine.

Reference:
(https://www.theguardian.com/culture/2002/nov/22/artsfeatures8)

789.

DDT is still used today to fight Malaria-spreading mosquitos, however, mosquitos are developing a tolerance to DDT.

Reference:
(https://www.ncbi.nlm.nih.gov/pmc/articles/PMC2801202/)

790.

Quincy Jones said in an interview that Marlon Brando had drug-influenced sexual relations with Richard Pryor, James Baldwin and others; Pryor's widow has confirmed this.

Reference: (https://www.theguardian.com/film/2018/feb/08/richard-pryor-and-marlon-brando-were-lovers-pryors-widow-confirms)

791.

In the 2000 Paralympics, 10 out of 12 players in Spain's ID Basketball team were non-disabled, who pretended to have intellectual disabilities. The scandal was exposed after the Paralympics, when one of the players was revealed to be an investigative journalist.

Reference: (https://www.youtube.com/watch?v=Y5F_ha7d-PI&feature=youtu.be)

792.

All hard sugar-based candies will sparkle when broken or scraped in the dark.

Reference: (https://www.scientificamerican.com/article/candy-lightning/)

793.

A man hiking in Colorado scared off a mountain lion by yelling Seinfeld dialog at it.

Reference: (https://www.upi.com/Lion-scared-off-by-Seinfeld-line/76101058886050/)

794.

In 2008, Tim McLean was beheaded and cannibalized while riding a bus in Canada. The perpetrator, Vince Li, spent seven years in mental hospital, and was released in 2015, to a group home. He was granted a discharge in 2017. One of the first officers on the scene later committed suicide.

Reference: (https://en.wikipedia.org/wiki/Killing_of_Tim_McLean)

795.

Henry L. Simpson, Franklin D. Roosevelt's Secretary of War, personally removed Kyoto from the top of the atomic bomb target list in part because he had had his honeymoon there.

Reference: (https://en.wikipedia.org/wiki/Kyoto)

796.

Sperm whales are so named because of a substance in their skulls that resembles seminal fluid.

Reference: (https://en.wikipedia.org/wiki/Sperm_whale)

797.

Despite the widespread success of his song "The Lion Sleeps Tonight," Solomon Linda never received a cent of its royalties and died poor in 1962. He didn't even get a gravestone until 18 years after his death.

Reference: (https://en.wikipedia.org/wiki/Solomon_Linda)

798.

In 1895, U.K. Prime Minister William Gladstone founded a public library. Aged 85, he wheelbarrowed his personal collection of 32,000 books the ¾ mile between his home and the library. His desire, his daughter said, was to "bring together books who had no readers with readers who had no books."

Reference: (https://en.wikipedia.org/wiki/Gladstone's_Library)

799.

Koshik, an elephant in South Korea, learned to imitate human speech.

Reference:
(https://www.youtube.com/watch?v=vLUz7E5gU2c&feature=youtu.be)

800.

The Prince Rupert's Drop, created by dripping molten glass into cold water, is capable of shattering bullets on impact and withstanding the blow of a hammer. This "glass droplet" is characterized by its incredibly high residual stress.

Reference: (https://en.wikipedia.org/wiki/Prince_Rupert%27s_drop)

801.

Barry Manilow was the piano player in Bette Midler's first touring band.

Reference: (https://youtu.be/XvCWSqIEsIs)

802.

Corn is classified as a cereal grain, yet the ears of corn are considered fruit.

Reference: (https://en.wikipedia.org/wiki/Maize)

803.

While they were originally thought to be white with black stripes because of their white belly, zebras are actually black, where the pigment is activated, with white stripes, where the pigment is inhibited.

Reference: (https://animals.howstuffworks.com/mammals/zebra-stripes1.htm)

804.

The Lion King, originally titled King of the Jungle, resembles the Japanese anime "The Jungle Emperor" about a lion named Kimba as he matures and becomes king, but Disney never gave credit to Kimba's creator. Matthew Broderick thought they were connected when he signed to be the voice of Simba.

Reference: (https://en.wikipedia.org/wiki/Kimba_the_White_Lion)

805.

In 1964, the British army tested LSD on their marines, to test its potential as a non-lethal weapon.

Reference:
(https://www.youtube.com/watch?v=KWodyapGNxI&feature=youtu.be)

806.

Doctors were 13 percent more likely to prescribe an antibiotic in the 13th appointment of a day and 19 percent more likely by the 24th appointment. The data mirrors similar 2014 findings published in JAMA Internal Medicine and recently summarized in the New York Times.

Reference:
(https://online.epocrates.com/drugs/403507/Lunesta/Pharmacology)

807.

Gilbert Baker, the creator of the gay pride flag, described himself as "gay Betsy Ross."

Reference: (https://www.nytimes.com/2017/03/31/us/obituary-gilbert-baker-rainbow-flag.html)

808.

Carl Sagan was given a 2 million dollar advance for the novel "Contact." It was the largest advance ever given for a book that had not been written at the time.

Reference: (https://en.wikipedia.org/wiki/Contact_(novel))

809.

A non-citizen cannot be deported from the U.S. if they become a member of the Kickapoo Indian Tribe.

Reference: (https://www.uscis.gov/ilink/docView/AFM/HTML/AFM/0-0-0-1/0-0-0-20736/0-0-0-20753.html)

810.

On U.K. roads zig-zag lines indicate to motorists that they are approaching a pedestrian crossing. It is an offence to stop a vehicle within the lines except when stopping for pedestrians using the crossing.

Reference: (https://en.wikipedia.org/wiki/Zebra_crossing)

811.

The company that makes Nutella, Ferrero, is the world's largest consumer of hazelnuts, buying around 25% of global production in 2014.

Reference: (https://www.bbc.co.uk/news/magazine-27438001)

812.

Scotland voted England's football song "World in Motion" as the best football song.

Reference:(http://www.heraldscotland.com/arts_ents/13164885.Top_football_song__Love_s_Got_the_World_in_Motion/)

813.

Isa Lake in Yellowstone National Park is the only lake in the world that drains to 2 separate oceans.

Reference: (https://en.wikipedia.org/wiki/Isa_Lake)

814.

Stephen King wrote a story about a house maid that swallows a writer's semen so her child will have his talent.

Reference: (https://en.wikipedia.org/wiki/Dedication_(short_story))

815.

The roadrunner is a type of cuckoo.

Reference: (https://simple.wikipedia.org/wiki/Roadrunner#Species)

816.

Some species of ant's farm, herd and protect aphids. The aphids produce a sugary honeydew substance that the ants feed on and, in exchange, the ants protect the aphids from predators.

Reference:
(https://en.wikipedia.org/wiki/Protocooperation#Ants_and_aphids)

817.

The Snakehead fish, native to Asia and Africa, can survive out of water for up to four days by breathing air through its gills. This made it an Apex predator when it was introduced into Maryland waters around 2004.

Reference: (https://en.wikipedia.org/wiki/Snakehead_(fish))

818.

The gesture of commemorating the victory by lifting the trophy above the head came in 1958 when photographers asked Bellini, captain of the Brazilian team at the time, to lift the World Cup trophy so that they could get a better view of it.

Reference: (https://en.wikipedia.org/wiki/Hilderaldo_Bellini)

819.

The land of the Shire from the Lord of the Rings was directly lifted from Tolkien's childhood memories of the village of Sarehole. In addition, many other locales from Middle Earth were also inspired by the surrounding countryside, including the Two Towers and the Old Forest.

Reference: (http://www.countryfile.com/countryside/quest-middle-earth)

820.

The "Parking Garage" episode of Seinfeld was filmed on the sound stage. The audience bleachers, Jerry's apartment and the restaurant were removed, and mirrors were setup around the entire set to make the garage look bigger.

Reference:
(https://en.wikipedia.org/wiki/The_Parking_Garage#Production)

821.

The official name for donkey meat is "poopy."

Reference: (http://newsnetone.com/2017/03/china-consumes-300-kenyan-donkeys-a-day/)

822.

The Mountain Meadows Massacre was conducted by Mormons, under the approval of Brigham Young, which killed over 120 innocent people on their way to California. The LDS denies they're responsible for the killings, and blamed it on the Paiutes Indians.

Reference:
(https://en.wikipedia.org/wiki/Mountain_Meadows_Massacre)

823.

Three out of the top five costliest Atlantic hurricanes on record occurred in just the last year with the three storms totaling $282 billion in damage, more than twice the cost of Hurricane Katrina.

Reference:
(https://en.wikipedia.org/wiki/List_of_costliest_Atlantic_hurricanes)

824.

Ulysses S. Grant was broke and dying of throat cancer, when Mark Twain offered an unheard of 75% of royalties to his widow for him to write his memoirs. Julia Grant received $450,000 dollars from royalties.

Reference: (https://en.wikipedia.org/wiki/Ulysses_S._Grant)

825.

The "Magic Relationship Ratio," according to science, states that for every negative interaction during conflict, a stable and happy marriage has five, or more, positive interactions.

Reference: (https://www.gottman.com/blog/the-magic-relationship-ratio-according-science/)

826.

In 1964, retiree Walter Seifert attacked and killed pupils and teachers at a catholic elementary school in Cologne with a flamethrower and lance.

Reference:
(https://en.wikipedia.org/wiki/Cologne_school_massacre)

827.

In 1953, anti-communist Mašin brothers, aged 20 and 22, conducted guerrilla operations in Czechoslovakia. They fled, fighting, shooting and narrowly escaping the largest manhunt ever in East Germany to cross the Berlin Wall. They later joined the U.S. Special Forces.

Reference:
(https://en.wikipedia.org/wiki/Josef_and_Ctirad_Ma%C5%A1%C3%ADn)

828.

An unsupervised "cold-turkey" approach to alcohol dependency can have severely adverse and fatal effects. Alcohol withdrawal symptoms such as seizures, Delirium Tremens, Korsakoff Syndrome, neurological difficulties and more can occur starting as early as 6 hours after peak intoxication.

Reference: (https://pubs.niaaa.nih.gov/publications/arh22-1/61-66.pdf)

829.

One of the earliest AIDS patients, Gaetan Dugas, was hunted down by one of his partners he infected. Dugas' charm proved unfailing: he sweet-talked the man into having sex again.

Reference:
(http://content.time.com/time/magazine/article/0,9171,145257,00.html)

830.

Alligators and crocodiles can climb trees.

Reference: (https://www.huffingtonpost.com/entry/alligator-in-tree-photo_us_577ec698e4b0c590f7e8aa6e)

831.

At the end of the 1979 NFL season, Hall of Fame Line Backer Jack Youngblood played three playoff games, including the Super Bowl, and the Pro Bowl with a fractured left fibula.

Reference: (http://www.talkoffamenetwork.com/broken-leg-didnt-keep-youngblood-pro-bowl/)

832.

Egypt invented taxes.

Reference: (https://en.wikipedia.org/wiki/Tax)

833.

The thousand-year old Bamiyan Buddhas of Afghanistan were destroyed by the Taliban in 2001, purportedly to protest the international aid given to preserving them.

Reference: (https://en.wikipedia.org/wiki/Buddhas_of_Bamiyan)

834.

In 1993, an American spelunker found evidence of people living in 2 Ukrainian caves during World War II. It was 1942, when a group of families survived the Holocaust by seeking refuge in the caves. Nearly 2 years later, someone left a bottled message alerting all of them the area was safe from Nazis.

Reference:(https://news.nationalgeographic.com/news/2004/05/0527_040527_grottosurvivors.html)

835.

For 70 years after the surrender of Vicksburg to the Union army on the Fourth of July, 1863, Independence Day wasn't celebrated in Vicksburg.

Reference: (http://www.todayinmississippi.com/mississippi_seen/article/3443)

836.

Grease 2 was meant to be the second film in a 4 film franchise. However, plans were scrapped after the movie bombed. Disney ended up adapting the unused script for Grease 3, which became High School Musical.

Reference: (https://screenrant.com/high-school-musical-movie-dark-secrets-trivia-facts/)

837.

M. Night Shyamalan's "Split" was based on outtakes from his 1999 movie "Unbreakable."

Reference: (http://ew.com/movies/2017/01/20/split-m-night-shyamalan-ending-interview/)

838.

"It's a Mad, Mad, Mad, Mad World" was known as "It's a Wonderful, Wonderful, Wonderful, Wonderful Bonanza" by stuntmen in Hollywood because of the sheer number of stunts performed in the film.

Reference: (http://www.philsilversshow.com/stunts)

839.

President Zachary Taylor died after eating copious amounts of raw fruit and iced milk.

Reference:
(https://en.wikipedia.org/wiki/Zachary_Taylor?wprov=sfti1)

840.

The National Responsible Fatherhood Clearinghouse officially endorses Dad Jokes.

Reference: (https://www.fatherhood.gov/dad-jokes/jokes)

841.

The noise from a finger snap sound comes from the middle finger hitting the meat of the palm near the base of the thumb at speed, not from the friction between the digits.

Reference: (https://en.wikipedia.org/wiki/Finger_snapping)

842.

Mosquitoes can continue to fly in the rain by redirecting the force of the impact with the drop.

Reference: (https://www.popsci.com/science/article/2013-06/fyi-how-do-mosquitoes-survive-rainstorm)

843.

Alfonso Ribeiro and Tatyana Ali appeared as their "Fresh Prince of Bel-Air" characters, Carlton and Ashley Banks, in a crossover episode with the sitcom "In the House".

Reference: (https://en.wikipedia.org/wiki/The_Fresh_Prince_of_Bel-Air#Crossovers_and_other_appearances)

844.

In 1985, the New Orleans Recreation Department held a party for its lifeguards, to celebrate their first drowning-free swimming season. A guest at the party drowned.

Reference: (https://www.nytimes.com/1985/08/02/us/victim-at-lifeguards-party.html)

845.

The President, or someone with and linked to the President, always carries a briefcase nicknamed the "football" that contains highly classified information dealing with nuclear launches and also serves as a communication device between the President and the Pentagon.

Reference: (https://www.smithsonianmag.com/history/real-story-football-follows-president-everywhere-180952779/)

846.

The first U.S. paperback edition of The Princess Bride featured a swords-and-sorcery style Princess Buttercup. It was so wrong for the book that the print run was stopped early and an all-text cover quickly substituted.

Reference: (https://io9.gizmodo.com/5894777/the-princess-brides-confounding-book-cover-and-other-ways-it-differed-from-the-movie)

847.

Steve Aoki's father was the founder of Benihana, hall of fame wrestler, porn magnate and off shore power boat racer worth $100 million at the time of his death.

Reference: (https://thehustle.co/rocky-aoki-benihana-family-fortune/)

848.

Hugh Thompson Jr. ordered his own crew to fire upon friendly soldiers if they wouldn't stop shooting civilians in the My Lai Massacre.

Reference: (https://youtu.be/E16O_Tlxs9s)

849.

The "Nader Bolt" is the bolt on vehicles that allows a hinged door to remain safely latched. It is named after Ralph Nader, who in his 1965 book "Unsafe at Any Speed" claimed that operator safety of American cars were fundamentally flawed.

Reference: (https://en.wikipedia.org/wiki/Latch#Automobiles)

850.

In 1957, Tulsa, Oklahoma, buried a Plymouth Belvedere to commemorate Oklahoma's 50th anniversary. In addition, citizens entered guesses as to what Tulsa's population would be in 2007, with the closets person winning the car. When the vault was opened it was filled with water and the car was ruined.

Reference: (https://blog.amsoil.com/story-of-miss-belvedere-brings-back-memories-of-tulsa/)

851.

White Castle restaurants are designed to mimic Chicago's historic water tower.

Reference: (https://en.wikipedia.org/wiki/White_Castle_(restaurant))

852.

The world's longest fence is 3,488 miles and is intended to prevent dingos from entering southeastern Australia.

Reference: (https://www.atlasobscura.com/places/dingo-fence)

853.

The Spanish language band Gipsy Kings are actually French.

Reference: (https://en.wikipedia.org/wiki/Gipsy_Kings)

854.

Hannah Senesh, a poet and Jewish paratrooper during World War II, flew from then Mandatory Palestine and infiltrated various European countries to organize resistance against the Third Reich.

Reference: (https://en.wikipedia.org/wiki/Hannah_Szenes)

855.

The long palmar muscle is a distinct ligament from the wrist downward when you make a fist, and about 14% of the population doesn't have it.

Reference: (https://en.wikipedia.org/wiki/Palmaris_longus_muscle)

856.

A dog's nose is as unique as a human's fingerprint and can be used to accurately identify them. The Canadian Kennel Club has been using this method to reunite owners with lost dogs since 1938.

Reference: (https://lostpetfinders.com.au/blog/did-you-know-dogs-noses-could-do-this)

857.

Jane Austin brewed her own beer. The Pride and Prejudice author's favored homebrew recipe included the buds of a spruce tree, which gave the beer citrus and pine flavors.

Reference: (https://vinepair.com/wine-blog/jane-austen-beer/)

858.

After the 2003 film "The Cat in the Hat" was released and panned by critics, the widow of Dr. Seuss vowed to never allow his work to be adapted in live action again.

Reference: (https://www.today.com/popculture/seussentenial-100-years-dr-seuss-2D80556399#.U9PpieNdU6s)

859.

The hit MGMT song "Me and Michael" got its name after the band wrote the song as "Me and My Girl" but decided it sounded too generic.

Reference: (https://en.wikipedia.org/wiki/Me_and_Michael)

860.

Despite reaching numbers of ten trillion or higher during devastating swarms in the 1870s, the Rocky Mountain locust went extinct less than 30 years later. It is still unknown why this species disappeared so rapidly.

Reference: (https://en.wikipedia.org/wiki/Rocky_Mountain_locust)

861.

In 1977, Aerosmith considered hiring a Convair CV-240 for use but rejected it as their assistant chief of flight operations doubted the vehicle's flight worthiness. That plane crashed on October 20, 1977, from fuel exhaustion due to poor maintenance, killing three members of Lynyrd Skynyrd.

Reference: (https://www.rollingstone.com/music/music-features/remembering-lynyrd-skynyrds-deadly-1977-plane-crash-2-195371/)

862.

The mom of Monty Python's John Cleese had such a temper that his, "Dad, who had fought in the First World War for three and a half years, sometimes yearned for the relative tranquility of the trenches."

Reference: (https://www.npr.org/2014/12/16/371179347/early-on-comedian-john-cleese-says-he-had-good-timing-but-little-else)

863.

A mosquito's mouth has 6 needles that's used to suck blood from our skin.

Reference: (https://www.npr.org/sections/health-shots/2016/06/07/480653821/watch-mosquitoes-use-6-needles-to-suck-your-blood)

864.

In order to get the look and feel of "Finding Nemo's" characters and world just right, Pixar's art team was required to take courses in marine biology, oceanography, and ichthyology in addition to enrolling in scuba diving classes.

Reference: (http://mentalfloss.com/article/64833/15-things-you-might-not-know-about-finding-nemo)

865.

In Gilbertese, the word for dog is "kamea," taken from Europeans who would tell their dogs "come here."

Reference: (https://en.wikipedia.org/wiki/Kiribati#Languages)

866.

The Limair Sanatorium in Luray, Virginia, was cooled by cave air from the Luray Caverns, making it the first building with air conditioning in 1901.

Reference: (https://www.atlasobscura.com/articles/limair-sanatorium-luray-caverns-air-conditioning)

867.

William Daniels, the actor who portrayed Mr. Feeny on "Boy Meets World," starred as John Adams in the Broadway musical and movie.

Reference: (http://www.playbill.com/article/lin-manuel-miranda-and-william-daniels-talk-hamilton-1776-mr-feeny-and-more)

868.

Under Arizona's "Stupid Motorist Law," if you become stranded after driving through barricades to enter a flooded road, you will be charged for your emergency rescue.

Reference: (https://www.phoenix.gov/fire/safety-information/onthemove/motorist)

869.

Stevie Nicks was absent during the original recording of Fleetwood Mac's hit, "Big Love". The "female" "ahh" during the "oh-ahh" vocal exchange, which many assumed to be Nicks, is actually Lindsey Buckingham, who sampled and altered his voice to mimic that of a woman.

Reference:
(https://en.wikipedia.org/wiki/Big_Love_(Fleetwood_Mac_song))

870.

Leonardo DiCaprio and Kate Winslet paid the care home fees of the last survivor of the Titanic.

Reference: (https://heatworld.com/celebrity/news/know-leonardo-dicaprio-kate-winslet-paid-care-home-fees-last-survivor-titanic-actual-guttural-sob/)

871.

The F-11 Tiger, during flight tests, managed to shoot itself down with 20 millimeter rounds fired from his own cannon.

Reference:
(https://www.popularmechanics.com/military/aviation/a27967/the-fighter-plane-that-shot-itself-down/)

872.

Gary Ridgway "Green River Killer" was forgiven by the father of one of his victims.

Reference: (https://www.youtube.com/watch?v=NmOUAdLgN1A)

873.

Farmer Fred Tuttle won the 1998 Republican primary for Vermont senator. He would ask his opponent, a millionaire "carpetbagger" from Massachusetts, questions at debates that only Vermonters would know. Tuttle would endorse his Democrat opponent of whom Tuttle said, "He knows how many tits on a cow."

Reference:
(https://en.wikipedia.org/wiki/Fred_Tuttle#Life_and_career)

874.

The HMT Rohna was the first troopship sunk in World War II by a German radio-guided "glide bomb." Over 1000 people perished, and the details were classified for decades.

Reference: (https://www.history.com/news/a-calamity-at-sea-70-years-ago)

875.

In 1935, a British engineer named Robert Watson-Watt was working on a weapon that would destroy enemy aircraft with radio waves. This weapon later evolved into Radar.

Reference:
(https://en.wikipedia.org/wiki/Radar#Just_before_World_War_II)

876.

The English word "girl" first appeared during the Middle Ages between 1250 and 1300 CE and originally meant a child of either sex.

Reference: (https://en.wikipedia.org/wiki/Girl#Etymology)

877.

Montana has the most extreme temperature range experienced in any of the 50 states.

Reference:
(http://montanakids.com/facts_and_figures/climate/Temperature_Extremes.htm)

878.

Francesco "Frank" A. Lentini had three legs, four feet and two sets of genitals due to being with a parasitic twin he absorbed in the womb. He even married in 1907 and had 4 children.

Reference: (https://en.wikipedia.org/wiki/Frank_Lentini)

879.

Bruce Bridgeman, a professor of psychology, lived 67 years stereo blind, unable to perceive depth. However, watching a 3D movie caused some changes in his brain's vision center that enabled him to experience stereoscopic three dimensional vision.

Reference: (https://www.theguardian.com/film/2013/jun/17/3d-movie-hugo-improves-mans-vision)

880.

During the Welsh revival of 1904, the donkeys in the mines had to be retrained because the miners no longer swore.

Reference: (http://www.moriahchapel.org.uk/index.php?page=1904-revival)

881.

In September, 2016, a 70 year-old Kansas man robbed a bank so he could get arrested, and get away from his wife.

Reference: (https://www.reuters.com/article/us-kansas-bankrobber-idUSKCN11D2KX)

882.

The Japanese have created talking body pillows. Groping the breast or crotch area causes responses such as, "What if I start loving you even more than I already do?" or if you squeeze too hard, "Hey! That hurts!"

Reference: (https://www.animenewsnetwork.com/interest/2016-03-16/interactive-rubbing-activated-hug-pillows-finally-get-release-date/.99866)

883.

The cell phone was invented by a Brazilian priest.

Reference:
(https://en.wikipedia.org/wiki/Roberto_Landell_de_Moura)

884.

Croatia tried to replace "hello" with "prepared", going to such lengths as to randomly call and monitor who had implemented the change.

Reference:
([https://en.wikipedia.org/wiki/Za_dom_spremni#CITEREFYeomans](https://en.wikipedia.org/wiki/Za_dom_spremni#CITEREFYeomans2013)2013)

885.

Since the onset of Colony Collapse Disorder in 2006, the number of U.S. honeybee hives is at a 20-year high and U.S. honey production is at a 10-year high.

Reference: (https://fee.org/articles/the-myth-of-the-bee-pocalypse)

886.

In order to link their Stone Age village to the outside world, 13 Chinese villagers carved their way through a mountain. Today, that tunnel is a tourist attraction.

Reference: (https://en.wikipedia.org/wiki/Guoliang_Tunnel)

887.

The colors of the NBC peacock represents the 6 divisions of the network which is news (Yellow), sports (Orange), entertainment (Red), stations (Purple), network (Blue), and productions (Green).

Reference:
(https://en.wikipedia.org/wiki/Logo_of_NBC#Adaptations)

888.

Harper Lee and Truman Capote were childhood friends who wrote together after school. To Kill a Mockingbird's character Dill is based on Capote. Lee was an "assistant researchist" for Capote to help write his book "In Cold Blood." Both of them spent two months conducting interviews for the book.

Reference: (https://www.rd.com/culture/harper-lee-to-kill-a-mockingbird-facts/)

889.

The pictures most often associated with the Rosa Parks incident were taken a year later from when she refused to give up her seat.

Reference: (https://www.nytimes.com/2005/12/07/nyregion/the-man-behind-rosa-parks.html?pagewanted=all)

890.

The BIPM doesn't use a physical rod that's exactly 1 meter similar to the physical "Kilogram" specimen, instead it uses a concise measurement of light and time defined in 1984 by the CGPM as the distance light travels, in a vacuum, in 1/299,792,458 seconds with time measured by a cesium-133 atomic clock.

Reference: (https://physics.nist.gov/cgi-bin/cuu/Info/Units/meter.html)

891.

Until the 18th century, the English Channel had no fixed name either in English or in French.

Reference:
(https://en.wikipedia.org/wiki/English_Channel#Ancient_references)

892.

After learning of Martin Luther King's death, Robert F. Kennedy delivered a speech in the, "heart of the African-American Ghetto of Indianapolis," informing the people of his death and attempting to keep the peace, as well. Indianapolis was one of the few cities that did not riot that night, thanks in part to his speech.

Reference:(https://en.wikipedia.org/wiki/Robert_F._Kennedy%27s_speech_on_the_assassination_of_Martin_Luther_King_Jr.)

893.

Prince recorded the synthesizer solo for "When Doves Cry" at half-speed and an octave lower against a half-speed backing track, speeding it up to create the final version. Keyboardist Matt Fink was tasked with learning and performing it at full speed live.

Reference: (https://www.vibe.com/2014/06/purple-rain-turns-30-revolutions-dr-fink-breaks-down-princes-classic-track-track/dr-fink-breaks-down-prince-purple-rain-track-by-track-2/)

894.

The Ark of the Covenant is claimed to be contained at the Church of Our Lady Mary of Zion in Ethiopia.

Reference:
(https://en.wikipedia.org/wiki/Church_of_Our_Lady_Mary_of_Zion
)

895.

Eating poppy seeds before having a drug test can make it test positive for opium.

Reference: (https://www.drugfoundation.org.nz/matters-of-substance/november-2014/mythbusters-poppy-seeds/)

896.

Mafia birds lay eggs in other birds' nests. Upon the detection and rejection of their egg, the host's nest is depredated upon, its nest destroyed and nestlings injured or killed.

Reference:
(https://en.wikipedia.org/w/index.php?title=Brood_parasite#Mafia_hypothesis)

897.

Eskimo is a term not only for the Inuit but also for the Inupiat and the Yupik. So it is not wrong calling Inuit people Eskimo.

Reference: (https://en.wikipedia.org/wiki/Eskimo)

898.

By 1991, the air in Mexico City had become so contaminated with fecal dust from humans that it was possible to contract hepatitis by simply breathing outdoors.

Reference: (https://www.nytimes.com/1991/05/12/world/mexico-city-s-toxic-residue-worsens-already-filthy-air.html)

899.

Since 1948, by state law in Connecticut, a pickle has to bounce to be considered a pickle.

Reference: (https://libguides.ctstatelibrary.org/law/pickle/resources)

900.

Poo-phoria occurs when your bowel movement stimulates the vagus nerve, which descends from the brain stem to the colon. It takes a particularly "large mass of stool" to trigger poo-phoria and its vagal-nerve-induced feelings of exhilaration, intense relaxation, and goose bumps.

Reference: (https://www.outsideonline.com/1784611/why-does-it-feel-good-poop)

901.

Rapper Lil Jon had a winery named "Little Jonathan Winery" located in the Central Coast of California.

Reference: (https://www.acquiremag.com/lifestyle/little-jonathan-winery)

902.

In the U.K. "child-like in nature" cartoon characters are banned from slot-machines because of more than 25,000 children under 16 that are considered problem gamblers.

Reference: (https://www.topratedbingosites.co.uk/multi-million-bingo-industry-analysis/)

903.

Germany does not extradite German citizens which is why Florian Homm, a hedge fund manager who the U.S. sentenced to 225 years in jail for ripping off his investors for hundreds of millions of dollars, is currently living in self-imposed exile in Germany to avoid extradition.

Reference: (https://en.wikipedia.org/wiki/Florian_Homm)

904.

Bebop Jazz rose in popularity partly due to a 20% "Cabaret Tax" in the 1940s, taxing any nightclub with singing or dancing.

Reference:
(https://www.npr.org/sections/ablogsupreme/2013/04/16/177486309/how-taxes-and-moving-changed-the-sound-of-jazz)

905.

A common treatment for methanol or wood alcohol poisoning is to give ethanol intravenously as it prevents the methanol from being converted to formaldehyde. This is because ethanol competes with methanol at the enzyme that breaks them down.

Reference: (https://en.wikipedia.org/wiki/Methanol_toxicity)

906.

Michael Jackson didn't like Eminem, because he parodied him in one of his songs and said that "good artists don't do that".

Reference: (https://youtu.be/rKE1Sc0wPLE)

907.

The terms Alien Hand Syndrome and Dr. Strangelove Syndrome refer to a variety of clinical conditions in which a person experiences their limbs acting seemingly on their own. It usually affects the left hand.

Reference: (https://en.wikipedia.org/wiki/Alien_hand_syndrome)

908.

Scousers are named after a stew called lobscouse, which was associated with Liverpudlian sailors.

Reference:
(https://www.theguardian.com/notesandqueries/query/0,5753,-6353,00.html)

909.

During the Sankebetsu Incident a brown bear repeatedly attacked a Japanese village and killed 7 people in 5 days. Today, it's still considered the worst bear attack in human history.

Reference:
(https://en.wikipedia.org/wiki/Sankebetsu_brown_bear_incident)

910.

SawStop is a safety device that will stop a table saw on contact with skin. Inventor Steve Gass tested it on his own finger, receiving only a scratch.

Reference:
(https://www.youtube.com/watch?v=6wtdUfZGfMg&feature=youtu.be&t=180)

911.

The Federal Reserve Bank of New York Building, in Lower Manhattan, serves as the largest gold repository in the world, holding approximately 7000 tons of gold bullion on behalf of the U.S. government, the IMF, and the central banks of 36 foreign nations.

Reference:
(https://en.wikipedia.org/wiki/Federal_Reserve_Bank_of_New_York_Building)

912.

Arctic foxes don't start shivering until -94 °F or -70 °C.

Reference: (https://en.wikipedia.org/wiki/Arctic_fox#Adaptations)

913.

Owls are known for their silent flight. Where other birds have stiff feathers that make a whooshing sound when they fly, owl feathers have soft edges that allow the birds to fly silently. This is important for owls, as they can swoop down on prey without being heard.

Reference: (http://justfunfacts.com/interesting-facts-about-owls/)

914.

The mudskipper is a fish that lives on land. It breathes air, uses its fins to walk on land, and even jumps in the air to attract mates. They also dig burrows underground to lay their eggs.

Reference:
(https://www.youtube.com/watch?v=KurTiX4FDuQ&feature=youtu.be)

915.

During the first modern Olympic Games in Athens, Greece, in 1896, there was just one winner who was rewarded with an olive wreath and a silver medal. The 1904 Olympic Games in St. Louis were the first in which gold, silver and bronze medals were gifted to the 3 winners.

Reference: (https://www.olympic.org/olympic-medals)

916.

The Blue Whale is not the largest animal to ever roam the Earth. Patagotitan, discovered in 2014, beats it by 7 meters in length.

Reference: (https://en.wikipedia.org/wiki/Patagotitan)

917.

The show "Time Team" was the biggest funder of archaeological digs in the United Kingdom.

Reference: (https://en.wikipedia.org/wiki/Time_Team)

918.

The tabletop RPG Dread uses Jenga instead of dice for conflict resolution. If the tower falls, you die.

Reference: (https://en.wikipedia.org/wiki/Dread_(role-playing_game))

919.

Vatican City's main imports include petroleum; medication; human blood; hard liquor; rolled tobacco; vacuum cleaners and butter.

Reference: (https://atlas.media.mit.edu/en/profile/country/vat/)

920.

In 1939, Russian minister Vyacheslav Molotov claimed bombing missions over Finland as humanitarian food deliveries for their starving neighbors. The Finns dubbed them "Molotov bread baskets". When the firebomb was developed, the Finns called it "Molotov cocktail", as "a drink to go with the food."

Reference: (https://en.wikipedia.org/wiki/Molotov_cocktail)

921.

Tour De France competitors need to consume 5,000 calories or more per stage of the race in order to maintain performance and health.

Reference: (http://www.cyclingweekly.com/news/racing/tour-de-france/this-is-what-you-have-to-eat-to-compete-in-the-tour-de-france-182775)

922.

Germany is the largest importer of human and animal blood in the world.

Reference: (https://atlas.media.mit.edu/en/profile/hs92/3002/)

923.

The F-82 "Twin Mustang" fighter plane, designed to escort bombers thousands of miles to Tokyo, was literally two P-51 Mustangs joined at the wing. Both cockpits were fully functional, so one pilot could sleep while the other flew the plane on missions that could last up to 12 hours.

Reference: (https://en.wikipedia.org/wiki/North_American_F-82_Twin_Mustang#Design_and_development)

924.

The International Astronomical Union names all mountains on Saturn's moon Titan after mountains and characters from J. R. R. Tolkien's works.

Reference:
(https://en.wikipedia.org/wiki/List_of_geological_features_on_Titan
)

925.

1830's advertisements to entice people to move to Houston, Texas, show the town as a bustling port city nestled next to a range of mountains, despite the port not built yet and the closest mountain over 500 miles away.

Reference:
(https://www.houstonchronicle.com/local/history/article/Promise-and-a-few-fibs-launched-this-city-s-7730948.php)

926.

During its construction, the "Gateway Arch" in St. Louis had to be cooled down to counteract thermal expansion. Due to it being built in two parts, the two legs of the monument expanded, leaving no space for the keystone at the very top.

Reference: (https://en.wikipedia.org/wiki/Gateway_Arch)

927.

Grave robbers target Confederate soldiers in the United States. Items can be sold at high prices to antique collectors. Buttons from Confederate uniform can be sold for $150; full uniforms and medals can be sold for $500; swords used by generals can be sold for $20,000.

Reference: (https://www.havocscope.com/price-of-confederate-generals-sword-when-stolen-by-grave-diggers/)

928.

Black holes "spaghettify" any objects entering the black hole, stretching them out like spaghetti in a process called spaghettification.

Reference: (https://en.wikipedia.org/wiki/Spaghettification)

929.

In the early 20th century, a company called Nutex made condoms that glowed in the dark thanks to them being infused with a radioactive element.

Reference: (https://gizmodo.com/5869753/once-upon-a-time-we-used-radium-condoms-for-glow-in-the-dark-sex)

930.

Asgardia, the Space Kingdom, is an online group aiming to become an independent nation in space, have launched their own satellite and plan to colonize the Moon within 20 years.

Reference: (https://en.wikipedia.org/wiki/Asgardia_(nation))

931.

The wrath of the Mongolians was so feared that, according to tales, a lone Mongolian soldier could walk into a village and kill its inhabitants to his heart's content without anyone trying to resist him.

Reference: (http://www.mongolia-web.com/1203-mongol-military-tactics-and-organization/)

932.

A person with damage to the right brain hemisphere can develop a "joke addiction", a compulsive need to constantly make jokes.

Reference:
(http://blogs.discovermagazine.com/neuroskeptic/2016/02/28/7457/)

933.

Matthias Sindelar, one of the world's best football players from the 1930s, in Nazi-occupied Austria, refused to play a propaganda match and scored two goals against Germany and then victoriously danced in front of the Nazi loge.

Reference: (https://www.newstatesman.com/sport/2008/06/austria-sindelar-soccer-nazi)

934.

In 2002, researcher Andrew Balmford found that eight-year-old British children could identify 80% of Pokémon, but only 50% of common wildlife species.

Reference:
(https://en.wikipedia.org/wiki/Andrew_Balmford#Research)

935.

When Eisenhower planned to visit Japan in 1960, the government called on Yakuza bosses to lend tens of thousands of their men as security guards.

Reference: (https://apjjf.org/2012/10/7/Andrew-Rankin/3688/article.html)

936.

The official terms for a left-hand page and a right-hand page are verso and recto.

Reference: (https://en.wikipedia.org/wiki/Recto_and_verso)

937.

Creed's Scott Stapp tried to kill himself, jumping out of a hotel window in Miami Beach.

Reference: (https://www.miaminewtimes.com/music/fact-creeds-scott-stapp-tried-to-kill-himself-jumping-out-hotel-window-on-miami-beach-6459449)

938.

H.G. Wells, a British writer born in 1866, predicted inventions such as emails, phones and lasers.

Reference: (https://www.smithsonianmag.com/arts-culture/many-futuristic-predictions-hg-wells-came-true-180960546/)

939.

The term "Nazi" was originally used in Germany as a derogatory term for a peasant or farmer. The term was later used by German leftists as a slur towards the National Socialist party.

Reference: (https://en.wikipedia.org/wiki/Nazism#Etymology)

940.

There was a cancelled Kinect-based Saints Row beat 'em up game that was partially reused in UFC Personal Trainer.

Reference: (https://www.unseen64.net/2014/10/13/saints-row-cooler-cancelled-xbox-360-ps3/)

941.

When Paris got its first daily newspaper in 1777, London already had nearly three hundred daily newspapers.

Reference: (https://www.theparisreview.org/blog/2016/07/05/an-extraordinary-delivery-of-rabbits/)

942.

Fergie, previously HRH Sarah Ferguson, Duchess of York, is the creator of "Budgie the Little Helicopter."

Reference:
(https://en.wikipedia.org/wiki/Budgie_the_Little_Helicopter)

943.

Most young impala are born around mid-day as this is the safest time to give birth since most of their enemies are resting. Half of impala newborns are killed by predators within the first few weeks of life.

Reference: (https://onekindplanet.org/animal/impala/)

944.

13% of all cars in Mongolia are Toyota Priuses.

Reference: (https://www.theglobeandmail.com/globe-drive/news/industry-news/where-the-priuses-roam-why-the-hybrid-is-conquering-the-land-of-genghis-khan/article30348763/)

945.

Tom Cruise's career saved Ray-Bans from extinction. Business was tanking in the 1970s, so Ray-Ban signed a product placement deal for 60 films. "Risky Business," "Top Gun," and "Rain Man" all had Cruise wearing Wayfarers and Aviators, and sales went through the roof.

Reference: (https://en.wikipedia.org/wiki/Ray-Ban_Wayfarer#cite_note-fa-5)

946.

When The Brady Bunch ended, Maureen McCormick became a raging drug fiend who prostituted herself for drugs. During a five-year binge, McCormick would sleep with her cocaine dealer, Bill.

Reference: (https://radaronline.com/photos/brady-bunch-cast-secrets-scandals-photos/)

947.

The place where Hitler committed suicide is now a playground for children.

Reference: (https://www.vice.com/en_us/article/ppmexz/the-site-of-hitlers-suicide-is-now-a-playground)

948.

Actor Don Johnson was once stopped at the Germany/Swiss border with $8 billion worth of bearer bonds and was accused of money laundering.

Reference: (http://articles.latimes.com/2003/mar/13/local/me-johnson13)

949.

There is a wild cat in South America called "Geoffrey's Cat" or Leopardus geoffroyi, and it's nearly endangered.

Reference: (https://en.wikipedia.org/wiki/Geoffroy%27s_cat)

950.

Aerojet Dade was a rocket testing and development facility located less than 5 miles outside of the Everglades. It was abandoned in the late 1960s.

Reference: (https://www.abandonedfl.com/aerojet-dade/)

951.

Humans caught the common cold from camels.

Reference: (https://www.independent.co.uk/news/science/cold-camels-study-where-does-it-come-from-scientists-discover-mers-outbreak-a7198771.html)

952.

At the height of the 1980's, during the Japanese property bubble, the grounds of the Imperial Palace in Tokyo were said to be worth more than all of the real estate in California.

Reference: (https://en.wikipedia.org/wiki/Tokyo_Imperial_Palace)

953.

Tokyo's underground flood water diversion system was completed from 1992 to 2006. It was built to mitigate overflowing of the city's major waterways and rivers during rain and typhoon seasons.

Reference:(https://en.wikipedia.org/wiki/Metropolitan_Area_Outer_Underground_Discharge_Channel)

954.

A school in Bromley, England, once held a rock concert featuring some of their young pupils: A band called "The Little Ravens" with 12-year-old Peter Frampton on guitar, and "George and the Dragons" with lead singer David Bowie.

Reference: (https://en.wikipedia.org/wiki/Peter_Frampton)

955.

In the late 1960s, a group of libertarians attempted to create a new country on a boat near the Bahamas. The boat almost immediately sunk in a hurricane.

Reference: (https://en.wikipedia.org/wiki/Operation_Atlantis)

956.

Henderson Island is one of two raised coral atolls left whose ecosystems remain largely unaffected by human contact. Nonetheless, it has the highest density of plastic rubbish anywhere in the world because of the Pacific Gyre currents.

Reference:
(https://en.wikipedia.org/wiki/Henderson_Island_(Pitcairn_Islands))

957.

An Australian man by the name of Steven Bradbury won gold in speed skating at the Salt Lake City Olympic Games in 2002, because everybody ahead of him fell at the end of the final lap.

Reference: (https://www.youtube.com/watch?v=vN7ih576VYM)

958.

There is a 700 year old painting in an Austrian church that looks very similar to Mickey Mouse.

Reference:
(http://news.bbc.co.uk/cbbcnews/hi/world/newsid_2481000/2481511
.stm)

959.

In the 6 years between "I Want to Hold Your Hand" and "Let It Be," the Beatles had the number one single in the U.S. for a total of 59 weeks and number one album for 116 weeks. In other words, they had the top single one out of every six weeks and the top-selling album one out of every three.

Reference: (https://en.wikipedia.org/wiki/Beatlemania)

960.

Liam Cunningham, the actor that plays Davos Seaworth on "Game of Thrones," played Captain Crew in the G-Rated classic Warner Bros. movie "A Little Princess".

Reference:
(https://en.wikipedia.org/wiki/A_Little_Princess_(1995_film))

961.

The famous game mode "Call of Duty Nazi Zombies" was almost cancelled, due to the mode being rushed, unplanned and was far behind schedule for the release of Call of Duty: World at War.

Reference: (https://www.pcgamer.com/call-of-duty-world-at-wars-zombie-mode-was-almost-canceled/)

962.

"Spandex" is an anagram of "expands."

Reference: (https://en.wikipedia.org/wiki/Spandex)

963.

Robin eggs are blue for a good reason. The male robin responds to the color of the eggs depending on the shade of blue they are. The paler the eggs are, the less time will be spent on the chicks once they hatch. The darker the shade of blue and the male will feed the chick twice as much.

Reference: (https://youtu.be/8H3vKG6PpBk)

964.

The V-1 Flying Bomb is a cruise missile designed by Lusser and Gosslau which could fly at speeds of at least 400 miles per hour and carried a warhead which weighed 1000 kilograms.

Reference: (https://en.wikipedia.org/wiki/V-1_flying_bomb)

965.

The town of Schaffhausen in neutral Switzerland was accidentally bombed by the Allies during the Second World War after being mistaken for the German city of Ludwigshafen am Rhein.

Reference: (https://www.swissinfo.ch/eng/schaffhausen-bombed_70th-anniversary-of-mistaken-us-attack/38278804)

966.

Before landing Spock, Leonard Nimoy got steady work acting as a thug "heavy" enforcer, using switchblades and guns to intimidate and beat people.

Reference:
(https://en.wikipedia.org/wiki/Leonard_Nimoy#Before_and_during_
Star_Trek)

967.

Damascus, Jericho, Aleppo, and Athens are the oldest continuously inhabited cities in the world.

Reference: (https://www.mnn.com/lifestyle/eco-tourism/stories/12-oldest-continuously-inhabited-cities)

968.

The world's most expensive bed, Baldacchino Supreme, costs $6.3 million.

Reference: (https://luxatic.com/the-top-10-most-expensive-beds-in-the-world/#1_Baldacchino_Supreme_Bed_8211_63_million)

969.

The Dahala Khagrabari was a piece of Bangladesh that was inside a piece of India, which itself was inside of Bangladesh.

Reference: (https://en.wikipedia.org/wiki/Dahala_Khagrabari)

970.

MOOSE was a proposed emergency "bail-out" system capable of bringing a single astronaut safely down from Earth orbit to the planet's surface that placed an astronaut in a bag which would fill with foam.

Reference: (https://en.wikipedia.org/wiki/MOOSE)

971.

Women in the U.S. do not have a constitutional right to equality. There was an Equal Rights Act introduced in the 1920s, but failed to be ratified in the 1970s by the 38 states needed to pass.

Reference: (https://unladylike.co/episodes/020/equal-rights-amendment)

972.

Dennis Rodman grew 10 inches in college and didn't play basketball before then.

Reference: (http://www.allheight.com/2012/12/late-growth-spurts-nba-players-tall.html?m=1)

973.

While Neil Armstrong was walking on the Moon, the Soviet Union had an unmanned spacecraft in lunar orbit on a mission to obtain soil samples. It crashed on the Moon the day Apollo 11 left.

Reference: (https://en.wikipedia.org/wiki/Luna_15)

974.

A man who survived a jump from the Golden Gate Bridge broke his back on impact, but was saved from drowning by a sea lion who kept him afloat until rescuers could reach him.

Reference: (http://www.abc.net.au/news/2015-03-03/suicide-survival-golden-gate-sea-lion-nsw-police-conference/6278280)

975.

A recent study also demonstrated that gut bacteria can produce significant amounts of amyloid and lipopolysaccharides, which are key players in the pathogenesis of Alzheimer's disease.

Reference:
(https://www.ncbi.nlm.nih.gov/pmc/articles/PMC5385025/)

976.

Cutter, a division of Bayer, knowingly sold blood tainted with the HIV virus to Taiwan, Malaysia, Argentina, China, and other "less developed countries", effectively infecting thousands of hemophiliacs with HIV.

Reference: (https://www.nytimes.com/2003/05/22/business/2-paths-of-bayer-drug-in-80-s-riskier-one-steered-overseas.html)

977.

Marvel censored M'baku's utterance of "Praise Hanuman!" in Indian releases of Black Panther, fearing that showing a seemingly villainous character praising a Hindu god would lead to backlash. Indians reacted highly negatively as they found that empowering rather than insulting.

Reference: (https://indianexpress.com/article/trending/trending-in-india/black-panther-fans-in-india-angry-over-beeping-out-hanuman-reference-twitter-reactions-5073987/)

978.

The makers of the "Airplane!" and "Naked Gun" movies bought a horse just to make a joke. They named the horse All Pink and instructed the jockey not to win but to stay on the inside rail the whole race just to hear the play-by-play announcer say "It's All Pink on the inside!"

Reference: (http://thelaughbutton.com/features/creators-airplane-pulled-off-one-funniest-jokes-weve-ever-heard/)

979.

NBA legend and Hall Of Famer Shaquille O'Neal made the largest purchase in Walmart history.

Reference: (https://youtu.be/-eNFUU7ea-Q)

980.

During the "Gold-Collecting Campaign" in South Korea, the general public donated personal treasures worth over $2 billion to help the country through the economic crisis of 1997.

Reference: (https://wikipedia.org/wiki/Gold-Collecting_Campaign)

981.

Medal of Honor Recipient Roy Benavidez had 37 puncture wounds and was pronounced dead until he spit in the face of the doctor who was trying to zip him up in a body bag.

Reference: (https://warhistoryonline.com/instant-articles/benavidez-vietnam-carried-onfighting-x.html)

982.

Cristiano Ronaldo's second given name, "Ronaldo" was chosen after U.S. president Ronald Reagan.

Reference:
(https://en.wikipedia.org/wiki/Cristiano_Ronaldo#Early_life)

983.

Human gene called ABCC11 prevents the armpit from producing an offensive odor. Roughly 2% of the population has this gene, mostly in East Asian populations.

Reference: (https://www.smithsonianmag.com/science-nature/a-lucky-two-percent-of-people-have-a-gene-for-stink-free-armpits-2508106/)

984.

Thanks to the General Mining Law of 1872, an individual miner could "patent" a claim on public land and buy it cheaply. As a result, in 1994 Utah was forced to sell public land worth up to $15 billion for only $26,487.

Reference: (http://www.kepstein.com/1994/05/22/federal-land-giveaway-fortune-under-the-desert/)

985.

There is a type of farming called vertical farming in which the farm is made in a multi-level building, which reduces waste and optimizes production. This type of farming could also help solve the epidemiological and environmental aspects of traditional farming.

Reference: (https://vertical-farming.net/)

986.

If you're a U.S. citizen living overseas, you can still vote in state and federal elections.

Reference: (https://www.overseasvotefoundation.org/)

987.

There are only 3 original citrus fruits: pommelo, citron and mandarin. Most other citrus fruits are hybrids of these 3.

Reference: (https://en.wikipedia.org/wiki/Citrus#Taxonomy)

988.

Sylvester Magee was both the last living former slave, last living Civil War veteran and oldest person ever. Born in 1841, and passing away in 1971, he was a slave until he fled to the north in 1863 and joined the Union Army, seeing action at Vicksburg and Champion Hill.

Reference: (http://allthatsinteresting.com/sylvester-magee)

989.

10 rivers in Asia and Africa do not contribute 90% of all the plastic trash in oceans; they actually contribute about 90% of the marine plastic trash originating from rivers.

Reference: (https://pubs.acs.org/doi/10.1021/acs.est.7b02368)

990.

Greenland is in North America.

Reference: (https://en.wikipedia.org/wiki/Greenland)

991.

The arena which is currently occupied by the Water World show at Universal Studios Hollywood used to house a Miami Vice themed show.

Reference: (http://www.thestudiotour.com/wp/studios/universal-studios-hollywood/theme-park/past-attractions/miami-vice-action-spectacular/)

992.

There are over 7500 varieties of apples known. It would take over 20 years for you to taste all of them if you ate an apple a day.

Reference: (https://en.wikipedia.org/wiki/List_of_apple_cultivars)

993.

A Texas man shot himself in the face after his bullet ricocheted of the armadillo he was trying to shoot.

Reference: (https://www.huffingtonpost.com/entry/texas-armadillo-shooting_us_59838ae2e4b08b75dcc5f622)

994.

Owning an electric car in Norway grants you free public parking, free ferry trips and the right to drive in bus lanes.

Reference: (https://elbil.no/english/norwegian-ev-policy/)

995.

Yoshi Shiratori successfully escaped from prison 4 times, including once when he rusted through his handcuffs with miso soup. After a year on the run, he turned himself back in and was finally paroled 20 years later.

Reference: (https://en.wikipedia.org/wiki/Yoshie_Shiratori)

996.

A rat king occurs when young rats living close to each other get their tails entangled and encrusted with dirt. This knot then tightens when they pull away from the group; the largest found comprised of 32 individual rats.

Reference: (http://www.guinnessworldrecords.com/world-records/66059-largest-rat-king)

997.

The "Mad Men" theme song was actually originally an unknown rap song by DJ RJD2 and rapper Aceyalone.

Reference: (https://mic.com/articles/87589/the-strange-origins-of-the-mad-men-theme-song#.tF08OgmF9)

998.

All the plants in Disneyland's Tomorrowland are edible. As Walt Disney meant to exhibit an "agrifuture" where humans make the most of their resources.

Reference:
(https://disneyland.disney.go.com/fr/disneyland/tomorrowland/)

999.

TV POWWW was an early interactive broadcast TV video game that had kids call in to a local station and shoot enemy space ships by yelling "pow" into their phone.

Reference: (http://mentalfloss.com/article/72420/80s-yelling-pow-your-tv-screen-could-win-you-happy-meal)

1000.

In 1989, a pilotless Soviet Air Force jet fighter crashed into a house in Belgium, killing one person. The pilot had ejected over an hour earlier over Poland after experiencing technical problems.

Reference: (https://en.wikipedia.org/wiki/1989_Belgium_MiG-23_crash)

www.ingramcontent.com/pod-product-compliance
Lightning Source LLC
Chambersburg PA
CBHW051253250726
48656CB00004B/1276